Praise
What Businesses Need

"*What Businesses Need to Know Right Now* is packed with great info from a variety of experts. It is an easy read, and I love that each section ends with the three top take-aways."

—Suzanne Moore

"Nettie Owens has compiled a treasure trove of wisdom from a diverse group of interviewees. Asking the right questions to experts in several fields, she has uncovered and cataloged valuable insights that will help the reader adjust to the world of COVID-19. Readable and relatable, this book will be useful long after the Pandemic is consigned to distant memory."

—Bruce M. Casner
CEO, Morgan Casner Associates, Washington, DC

"*What Businesses Need to Know Right Now* brings together a treasure trove of industry experts that deliver value on each and every single page. No matter where you are in business, the message is clear—opportunity is all around you, no matter what economic indicators may point to."

—Cat Stancik
The Founder of Action Incubator, Bestselling author of *7 Principles for a More Productive and Fulfilling Life* and creator of the Lead Boss System

"Nettie Owens has woven together insights from business leaders that can help us navigate, maneuver, and even grow our businesses during this unique time. Dive into this book to find key takeaways and strategies to move your business forward today."

—Cindy Sullivan
CPO, Owner—cbSullivan Consulting & Organizing and President, Institute for Challenging Disorganization

"As a small business owner, I was fascinated by the amount of information in these interviews which I look forward to modifying and then applying. This book will be a valuable resource for me, and others, for many years to come."

—Diane Quintana
Master Trainer, CPO-CD®, CPO® DNQ Solutions, LLC and Best-Selling Author

"This book is right on time and simultaneously timeless. These interviews in various business segments get you back to basics. In these short to the point master classes with leaders in their field cut the fluff and tells you 'What Businesses Need To Know.'"

—EJ Cutliff
Owner of Esoteric Sports Alliance & Host of the Black in Sports Podcast

"Nettie has this wonderfully effortless way of pulling loads of value out of the guests she interviews. It's as if her conversational style was meant for the printed page. I look forward to even more from her in the future!"

—Andrew Kap
Author of *The Last Law of Attraction Book You'll Ever Need To Read*

WHAT
BUSINESSES
NEED TO
KNOW
RIGHT NOW

Lessons Learned
From Interviewing Businesses
During a Pandemic

Fred,
Thank you
for contributing
your expertise to
help others succeed.
Nitta

WHAT BUSINESSES NEED TO KNOW

RIGHT NOW

Lessons Learned
From Interviewing Businesses
During a Pandemic

NETTIE OWENS
CPO-CD®

Table of Contents

Introduction 1

STRATEGY 5

A Marketing Plan Is A Living Document 9
A Business That's Representative of Who You Are 14
Blind Spots 19
Secret Weapons for Business 24
Opportunities Exist Everywhere 28
Revenue Kung-Fu 33
Adaptation in Delivering Medicine 37

SALES 41

Prepare for All Seasons 44
Start & Continue the Conversation 49
Don't Stop Selling 54
Create Your Conversion Equation 58

LEADERSHIP 63

Spiritual Leadership 67
Leadership Can (and Should) Be Taught 72
Engage in Transparency to Create True Partnership 77
Conscious Leadership 83

FINANCIAL 87

Create a Cash Flow Strategy 91
Integrating Business & Personal Finance 95
Allow Your Agent to Be a Trusted Advisor 100
Health Care Cost Containment 105
Do Your Research on Tax Strategies 109

COMMUNICATION 115

Defy the Status Quo 119
Build Relationships through Emotion 123
Clear, Consistent Communication 128
Be More Than a Walking Business Card 132
Storytelling through Podcasts 137
The Experience Economy 141

CONNECTION & COLLABORATION 145

Establish Partnerships 149
Virtual Networking 154
Utilize Emotional Brand Intelligence 158
Be Yourself on Camera 163
Build an Alchemy Network 167

PEOPLE 173

Recruiting 176
Hiring 180
Value Your People 184
Business & Mental Health 189

DIVERSITY, INCLUSION, EQUITY & BELONGINGNESS 195

Embrace Diversity to Build a Better Workplace 199
Be Interested and Listen 204
Be Willing to Converse 209
Creating a Safe Space for Conversation 216

PRODUCTIVITY & MINDSET 223

Focus on Physical Health 227
Adjust Your Mindset 232
Working with Your Life Partner 236
Tap into Your Natural Intuition 240
Lessons from ADHD 245
The Next Right Thing, for the Right Reasons, with the Right Heart 250
Mindset Is an Inside Job 255

TECHNOLOGY 261

Cybersecurity 264

Conclusion 268
Acknowledgments 271
About the Author 272

To My Family—You are my world.

The interviews compiled in this book were captured between April and September 2020. Each has been minimally edited for readability. You may assume that the words in the interview are those of the person being interviewed, and the text in italics as well as the questions are from the author.

Introduction

No one ever really believed it could happen, but the world stopped spinning.

Several months ago, the planet came to a slow, grueling halt, like the metallic grinding of a machine coming to rest.

And we all waited, pensively wondering what would happen next. Would we or our loved ones become ill? Would we die? Could we operate our businesses? What would happen to our children? What about school, childcare, grocery shopping? What should we do? Stay home? Go out? A million questions were spinning through our collective emotional atmosphere.

It was March 2020; the world was at a standstill from the global pandemic that had taken over every aspect of life. Businesses shut down overnight. Workforces were laid off or moved to work from home. Schools closed. Houses of worship shut their doors. Everything we had come to know as "normal" came into question.

And then, about six weeks later, plans were underway for us to return from isolation and begin interacting again. But the pandemic was not over, not even close, and there were more questions than answers in the daily news.

In a conversation I had with a fellow business consultant colleague, the query came up, "What is it that businesses and business owners need to know right now?"

I wanted to know what businesses need to know about reopening their doors, accommodating employees who were working at home alongside their partners, bringing their work-force back, or letting them continue to work from home.

What did businesses need to know about technology, leadership, branding, lead generation, and more? I wasn't looking for answers that required deep research and advanced study but what did we need to know right at this exact moment.

Selfishly, I sought first to get the answers I was seeking for myself. I started interviewing subject experts who had something to say beyond the Business 101 level, and who could speak to the challenges we were facing in that exact moment. What followed were daily, live broadcast, 10-minute conversations with leading voices in the entrepreneurial and business world. The interviews gained popularity, and I heard that people were watching the recordings one after another as I posted them. You can check out all the interviews here as the list continues to grow: WhatBusinessesNeedToKnow.com.

As I had one conversation after another, the fog began to lift, hope began to return, and the real answers I gathered helped business owners find their footing again. I discovered that even though the information being shared was relevant and specific to what we were experiencing during the pandemic, it also contained solid truths about good business practices that are timeless. At the encouragement of Jennifer McGinley, with JLM Strategic Communications, I pulled this information together into the volume you now hold.

This book organizes these valuable conversations by topic, including strategy; sales; leadership; finance; communication; connection and collaboration; people; diversity, inclusion, equity and belongingness; productivity; and technology. In each interview, I emphasize the bottom line of what you need to know right now, plus three key points or action items you can use. While you can read this book from cover to cover, you will also find value just by opening to a page and digesting one conversation at a time.

The interviews all happened in a bubble, a closed and confused world trying to survive the greatest global calamity in over a century. They also reflect the genuine experiences of those being interviewed. There are times when you will want to shout in frustration along with the expert, and other times when you will want to highlight passages and take notes about what to put in place next.

I hope you enjoy learning from these experts as much as I enjoy the opportunity to bring these conversations to you. I would love to hear from you! Join the conversation at WhatBusinessesNeedtoKnow.com and let me know what your favorite interviews were, along with what knowledge you will apply going forward.

To your success!

Nettie Owens

STRATEGY

A Marketing Plan Is a Living Document | 9
with Gerri Knilans

A Business That's Representative of Who You Are | 14
with Keri Herndon-Brown

Blind Spots | 19
with Keith Daw

Secret Weapons for Business | 24
with Scot MacTaggart

Opportunities Exist Everywhere | 28
with Ben Chai

Revenue Kung Fu | 33
with Erik Luhrs

Adaptation in Delivering Medicine | 37
with Dr. Ernesto Gutierrez

STRATEGY

Rowing harder doesn't help if the boat
is heading in the wrong direction.
—Kenichi Ohmae

The first lesson that businesses need to learn is that even in uncertainty, you start with a strategy. Begin with what you know and work out the plan from there. The reality is that the plan will change. But if you have set aside time for strategic planning, you will be able to grow with the change.

Gerri Knilans of Trade Press Services shares the importance of having a marketing plan that touches all aspects of the business. She outlines the exact steps to put this plan together and what you need to do to ensure its success.

Keri Herndon-Brown of Strategic Admissions Advice and Marriage, Family, Business, talks about the systems in your business and, from there, creating a business that is representative of who you are, who you are serving, and what you stand for.

Keith Daw of McDonell Consulting Group delves into the blind spots that we all have in our business because we are so close to it day-to-day. He expresses the importance of getting an outside perspective and to always be looking for your blind spots.

Scot MacTaggart of EagleDream Technologies encourage us to look for "secret weapons" in our businesses. These are innovations that you can prioritize for maximum impact. Analyzing your business makes identifying a secret weapon possible.

Ben Chai of Propertunities, who is an expert strategist, reminds us that opportunities exist everywhere that problems exist. Start with an understanding of what kind of business you are creating, and make sure that you know yourself and what strengths and challenges you bring to the table.

Erik Luhrs of Revenue Kung-Fu states that it is never too late to change direction or start over. Big moments, like those during the pandemic of 2020, can be an opportunity to let go of what's not working, slow down, and move forward with purpose.

Dr. Ernesto Gutierrez of Practice Growth Formula explores the opportunities for innovation and exponential growth that come with the need to solve problems quickly. Red tape that often stymies progress has largely been removed, and projects that were once seen as "nice to have" become the priority to solve now.

A Marketing Plan
Is A Living Document

Gerri Knilans
Co-Founder & President
Trade Press Services

Gerri helps companies and individuals accelerate business growth by increasing visibility in the marketplace, developing a competitive edge, communicating more effectively with customers and prospects, and gaining recognition as experts in their fields. With over 40 years of experience as a sales and marketing professional, entrepreneur, consultant, author, and educator, she has excellent credentials and a proven track record of success.

She is the president of Trade Press Services, a specialized marketing communications strategy firm that provides writing, media outreach, and general marketing support. Under her leadership, Trade Press Services has worked with more than 500 B2B clients, from start-ups to Fortune 500 companies and more than 750 editors of trade magazines, journals, newspapers, and other media outlets. Prior to joining Trade Press Services, she was a principal in a marketing consulting firm for 15 years.

Main Takeaway

Creating a robust marketing plan with a budget, responsibilities, and evaluation allows everyone to be involved and returns real results.

Questions

1. Why do so many companies not have a marketing plan? Why, after so many years, are companies trying to operate without a marketing plan?

2. What does a marketing plan do for a company?

3. What are the key components of a practical and actionable marketing plan?

Interview: What do businesses need to know right now about marketing communications?

Gerri Knilans serves B2B companies that are looking to grow and recognize that growth requires planning. The best kind of growth is planned for and evaluated. She helps clients expand their marketing outreach, increase visibility in their marketplaces, and develop recognition as a thought leader in their industry. Gerri is sharing what businesses need to know right now about marketing communications.

Why do so many companies not have a marketing plan? Why, after so many years, are companies trying to operate without a marketing plan?

I think it goes back to the old adage, "Failing to plan is planning to fail" (Benjamin Franklin). I think that there are a lot of CEOs who don't have marketing experience. They may be experts in their product or service, or in finance, but they're not marketers. And so they think that the process is something the salespeople should handle because they are responsible for bringing in the dollars. Or they think it's overwhelming. Or they think, "Well, I really do have a plan, but it's not written and communicated." Those are some of the reasons why companies don't have plans.

Are you finding that it's more important now, or kind of the same as usual? What is the relevance of creating that plan?

I think it's more important than ever, although it's always been important. It's a great opportunity to put everyone on the same page. And what marketing planning can do for you is to help the CEO and leadership team develop common goals, common visions, and common missions, and really get on the same page and understand what their roles and responsibilities are in contributing to the success of a company.

A marketing plan isn't something you do once a year. It's something you do, and you evaluate, and you monitor it on an ongoing basis so that you can tweak it and make changes. You can take corrective action. What better time than now in this COVID pandemic, when everything is turned upside down, to really be able to take a look at your plan and say, "Whoops! What's working? What's not working? What can we do more of? What should we do less of?"

I was going to ask you about the naysayers who say, "Well, we made a marketing plan, and then coronavirus and quarantine and everything happened. And now our plans are out the window." But you're saying a marketing plan is a living document. It's something that you use as a guide, but then you're adapting to the changes in the marketplace, looking at what's working and what's not working.

Really what it's about is a more collaborative effort. Sometimes the marketing plan is written by the marketing department, but what happens to the salespeople, the business development people, the customer service people, the product development people, the inventory management people? They should be contributing their thoughts and ideas and input and where they fit into marketing in general. Marketing isn't as dry and clear-cut as it once was.

Are there guidelines that we can go by on how to start this plan? Are there certain components that need to be part of the plan?

I think many people don't take the time to develop a comprehensive plan. That starts with putting the vision and mission down on paper, so everybody knows what you're trying to achieve, what you're in business to do. That's where it starts.

From there, you want to go to what your goals are and try and quantify them. Whether it's the number of new clients or customers, or the amount of repeat business, or the number of new marketplaces you're going to go into, you want to be able to quantify goals.

The next part of your marketing plan is the strategy. What strategies are you going to use to achieve each of the goals that you've set forth?

And then tactics. What are the individual activities, programs, and initiatives that will support each other and the strategies?

Most people start at the tactics, and that's where things begin to fall apart. What they haven't done is they haven't put a budget together for their marketing plan. If you have a marketing plan that is unfunded, of what value is it? You have a marketing budget, and then you look at your strategies; you may see that you have to revise.

A marketing budget has to be part of the process. After that, there's also the assignment of responsibilities. If you don't know who is responsible for each of those goals, strategies, and tactics, things can fall through the cracks. Assign responsibilities. There can be some teamwork and cross-department collaboration. Once you have your assignment of responsibilities, answer, "What are our first-quarter activities? What are our second-quarter activities? Third and fourth?"

Lastly, you have to monitor the plan. Plan on a monthly or bimonthly basis, and say, "How's it coming? What have we done? What's working? What isn't working? Let's go back to the drawing board." We have to not only hold one another accountable for our areas of responsibilities but also not point the finger when something goes awry. We get into problem-solving mode and roll up our sleeves on what we can improve. I think it's the last step—that budgeting, assignment of responsibility, scheduling, and calculation—that really puts the meat on the marketing plan to make it successful.

Companies run the gamut. You have folks who are simply at the whim of whoever shows up on their business doorstep and says, "I have advertising to sell you!" and then they buy it, and they don't have a plan. There are companies that have the outline of the plan that you talked about. But then they never get to that budgeting and assignment of responsibilities and follow-through that really makes it a living document, not something that you look at once a year. The plan needs that full scope.

Three Action Steps

1. Shift your perspective to understand the value of developing and maintaining a marketing plan.

2. Pull a team together to work on the plan so that every aspect of the company is reflected and people have buy-in.

3. Create the plan with a budget, responsibilities, and dates set to re-evaluate.

Connect with Gerri Knilans at www.linkedin.com/in/gerriknilans
or www.tradepressservices.com
for the Marketing Insights Newsletter.

A Business That's Representative of Who You Are

Keri Herndon-Brown
COO & CEO
Strategic Admissions Advice and Marriage, Family, Business

Keri Herndon-Brown is the COO of Strategic Admissions Advice, an educational consulting company that teaches parents how to help their child choose the right major, college, and career.

Main Takeaway

On all levels, your business should be representative of who you are, who you are serving, and what you stand for.

Questions

1. As a business owner, what are some of the things you saw as business owners went to apply for various grants and funding and loan options?

2. As a company that's owned by two people of color, what things are affecting your business? What do you think businesses need to know from that perspective?

3. What can companies be doing right now to assist college students?

Interview: What do businesses need to know right now about the hot topics that are currently unfolding?

Keri Herndon-Brown is the COO of Strategic Admissions Advice, an educational consulting company that teaches parents how to help their child choose the right major, college, and career. She founded it with her husband, Shereem Herndon-Brown, 15 years ago. She's been married for 20 years and is the mother of four amazing children. She's sharing what businesses need to know about the hot topics that are currently unfolding.

As a business owner, what are some of the things you saw as you went to apply for various grants and funding and loan options?

The main thing that I found out from people who didn't have their papers is that they needed their employee identification number (EIN) documented—which was something that the Paycheck Protection Program (PPP) required—and trying to call the IRS and get through wasn't happening.

Also, you had to have a business bank account. I heard from several people who always kept their personal accounts and never transferred over to a business account. So, that stopped them from moving ahead. You also needed some articles of organization. Obviously, your state paperwork had to be in order, and you had to have different business licenses. A lot of people didn't have that paperwork together.

Even as an established business, you want to make sure you have everything in order—so that if an emergency arises, you're not scrambling to get things together.

As a company that's owned by two people of color, what things are affecting your business? What do you think businesses need to know from that perspective?

Everyone needs to be empathetic right now and consider what you're posting on social media. A lot of people have automatic posts going out. Sometimes you have to reconsider the climate in which you're posting something. Something that could have been funny may not be now.

If you're going to stand in solidarity with either group, and again, I'm not telling you what side to choose, people need to take a stance and be willing to own that space. If you are a person for Black Lives Matter, or if you are on the opposite side with All Lives Matter, then make that known—this way, people can spend their money accordingly.

I also think it's important for us to realize that we have to diversify our companies across the board. Who are we? Who are we serving? Who's on our boards? Who's the head of the company? What do they stand for?

It's also important to understand this when it comes to social media. Not everyone should be talking for the company. Even as the owner of the company, you might not be the best voice to get your point across, because sometimes people will say things in the moment.

For example, Drew Brees posted on social media then saw how his words hurt his family and teammates. He had to come back and say something new. So, sometimes maybe running things by the internal office, or your PR and media team to say, "We want to make this statement, but it doesn't read the way we want to . . ." is a good idea. I always go back to: a joke written down doesn't always get a laugh when you say it out loud.

The World Economic Forum says that, "Empathy is a sustainability tool that can help us create a far better environment in which to live and work. It is both something we can learn how to use and a resource that we can use to learn."

What can companies be doing right now to assist college students?

You have the best opportunity right now as a business owner. Now you have thousands of high school students who are heading into college and regular current college students—at home. And you can do virtual internships for them.

So, maybe someone comes on to your PR and marketing team. You can allow them to come on via Slack and Google Hangouts and all of these other meetup opportunities and work with your PR team to get experience. You can have them join you and work on your website and your web design. It's a great opportunity for established business owners.

You want to make sure to be fair—that you're not really too much of a startup where they're not going to get the information and the opportunity they would normally get. Because remember—it's already skewed because they're not in the office with you. Someone's not sitting side by side with Nettie learning the ins and outs of your business. You want them to get the most exposure that they can, and make sure that you have someone that can handle that new task of managing. We have a great opportunity right now to bring on students and give them great exposure. We can help them through this process because their education just stopped.

If you're an established business, have you thought about the opportunity to offer someone an internship with you? What skills can you teach and share? What might an intern bring to you?

Three Action Steps

1. Ensure that you have established your business from a financial and legal perspective. (i.e., having your EIN, opening a business bank account, etc.).

2. Diversify your company on all levels to represent who you are, who you are serving, and what you stand for.

3. Consider bringing on an intern that you can share your skills and knowledge with, in turn helping them further their education.

Connect with Keri Herndon-Brown at
www.linkedin.com/in/kherndonbrown/
or strategicadmissionsadvice.com/contactus

Blind Spots

Keith Daw
Vice President of GSD & Trainer
McDonell Consulting Group

Keith Daw is the Vice President of GSD and Trainer at McDonell Consulting Group, an authorized licensee of Sandler Training. He places his focus and energy on amplifying professionals, teams, and organizations in the areas of leadership, sales, strategic customer care, and interpersonal communication.

Main Takeaway

Allow an outsider to take a look at your business and provide you with a review that highlights where your blind spots are and what you are doing well. Then work to fix those blind spots to take your business to the next level.

Questions

1. What are blind spots in business, and why do businesses need to start turning towards them?

2. How often should you get an outsider's perspective on your business?

3. What are some tools or resources that people can use to evaluate their business blind spots?

Interview: What do businesses need to know right now about blind spots?

Keith Daw places his focus and energy on amplifying professionals, teams, and organizations in the areas of leadership, sales, strategic customer care, and perhaps most importantly, human communication. During these times, human communication may be the most important thing, as some are doing it well right now, and others are struggling. Keith has so much to share, but let's dive into what do businesses need to know right now about blind spots.

What are blind spots, and why do businesses need to start turning towards them?

When it comes to the idea of blind spots, there's a saying, "What you don't know can kill you," and that's very applicable to business. There are lots of business owners who know what they do well, and they do a lot of it. Yet sometimes, as a business goes along, things are just kind of "created" in the moment and it's a bit like creating an airplane in the air. While it may be working at the moment, is it really working to its full potential? It's helpful to have a third party to look at what you're doing and bounce ideas around. Because there may be some gaps in there—some blind spots.

Whether it's with their people, their processes, or any of the metrics that a business may be measuring to achieve milestones and make adjustments, they may still experience blind spots. Perhaps you think your business is going well, but when a third party reviews it and looks at all of your metrics, they may find that you're maybe at 80 percent—and you don't know what it takes to get to that 100 percent. What's it going to take to get that last 20 percent?

To have that outside perspective that can audit your blind spots and provide some validation on what you're doing well is a great benefit to a business. It could be the needed push to get your business to the 100 percent level—and that's why you need to turn towards them.

There may be some fear in having an outsider look at your business and provide you with an unbiased critique; after all, you've worked hard to create your business. But know that the benefits can be enormous and bring light to those blind spots that you've not seen or ignored.

How often should you get an outsider's perspective on your business?

There is no simple answer to this question. Let's take a look at a couple of professions. If you're a CPA, a third party might be evaluating numbers quarterly. And if you're a lawyer with your own firm, you may automatically be doing a review with each contract that's put into place. But when it comes to the areas of business that involve people and processes and things such as sales, leadership, etc.—usually what happens is that help is sought when there's a problem or when there's a hiccup. At this time, a third party would be an asset to see what needs to be tweaked in a business to avoid problems in the future. And this may be reactive in nature to the current situation a business is facing or proactive in looking to the future to avoid problems.

An outside perspective can help you answer:

- Are there things that we've always done that we need to keep doing?
- Are there things that we've always done that perhaps we need to adjust?
- Do we need to do more of the same thing—but in a slightly different way than we did it before?
- Are there things that we need to get better at and improve upon?

While the scheduling or timing of an outsider to come review your business may vary from business to business, the importance of it exists for every business.

What are some tools or resources that people can use to evaluate their business blind spots?

McDonell Consulting Group has a complimentary bench-marking assessment that we share with business owners all the time. It's a tool that makes people pause and truly look at their business, probably in ways that they don't typically do. When they use this benchmark to assess their business, they may see that they're in the 66th percentile—which is not bad. They can then really think about the areas where they're perhaps focusing too much or too little of their time.

For example, I worked with a company that was growing extremely quickly. So quickly, in fact, that they had put people into leadership roles within the company that they may not have been prepared for. There was a lack of resources and personal and professional development for these leaders due to the fast growth of their business.

But then the company paused, and the owner said, "I don't know from a personal and professional development standpoint who's really slated to be an awesome leader." The owner wanted to know what to give them to be able to execute and succeed.

We used an assessment that focuses on competencies and aptitudes in leadership. And we evaluated the entire company.

Why the entire company? Why not just the leaders? The owner believed it would be good to know the competencies and aptitudes for everyone in his company for many reasons. The assessment helped to answer:

- What, if anything, do I need to do differently or better to provide resources for my leaders?

- Who are the people that I should have my eye on for future leadership roles when the need arises, and will they be ready for it?

- What am I doing to make certain that people are in the right roles and that I have them on the right path to success?

The owner explained to the company the challenges that they were facing from a leadership standpoint. He addressed the importance of fixing them now rather than waiting, so that the struggles would not continue or grow worse—costing the company employees or clients.

Being proactive when looking for blind spots in your business may be one of the most beneficial things you can do for your business.

Think of it like having a regular checkup with your doctor. You shouldn't just go to the doctor when you're sick. You should have those regular checkups to avoid serious health problems in the future. Getting an outside perspective on your business is a bit like preventative medicine.

Three Action Steps

1. Contact a third party or take Keith's business assessment and see where your blind spots are.

2. Correct those blind spots so that you can take your business to the next level.

3. Schedule third-party assessments of your business regularly to avoid problems in the future.

Connect with Keith at www.linkedin.com/in/keithdaw/ or if you're interested in receiving his benchmark assessment for your business, go to www.mcdonell.sandler.com/assessments_tools

Secret Weapons for Business

Scot MacTaggart
Regional Sales Director
EagleDream Technologies

Scot MacTaggart is the Regional Sales Director for EagleDream Technologies, where he works with cloud and software technology. He specializes in what he calls "secret weapons for business." Additionally, he's the host of the award-winning *Pitchwerks* podcast, which tackles everything from sales and marketing to account management and advertising.

Main Takeaway

In a world full of technology and innovation, the choices can be overwhelming. But when you decide on the priorities for your business, you can reduce your overwhelm and implement what works for you.

Questions

1. What is a secret weapon for business?

2. What's an out-of-the-box secret weapon you are seeing?

3. Once you've implemented these secret weapons, what should you do?

Interview: What do businesses need to know right now about secret weapons?

There is so much to know about business, but what if you could learn a few secret weapons? What you need to know right now about secret weapons for business is what Scot MacTaggart is going to share. At EagleDream Technologies, Scot helps businesses get to the next level by combining proven management techniques with the strategic use of technology.

What is a secret weapon for business?

With so much technology out there and available to businesses, it can be a daunting task to figure out what your business needs in the present and what it will need down the road.

Right now, there is an immeasurable number of choices that can help to innovate your business. In fact, there are so many available that there is no clear consensus about what people should be using, and we end up with a lot of buzzwords being thrown around. But the true secret weapon for a business is the ability to identify all of those different potential innovations.

What's an out-of-the-box secret weapon you are seeing?

Do you know what technology and innovations are important to you and your business right now? There are so many possibilities available that you may need to do your research and start a list of the ones that would be beneficial to your business and eliminate the ones not needed at the moment.

One of the most important secret weapons to be aware of right now is the ability to prioritize—and that's FREE. You need to adjust the way you think about the infinite buffet of choice you have. You have to think in terms of priority now. For example, is artificial intelligence valuable for a lot of businesses—if not all businesses? The answer is yes. But is it the number one priority for your business? Is it the number five priority? Is it number thirty on the list?

You need to be able to look at the innovations and technology and say, "This one's good for us. This one's not so good for us. This should be our first priority, and this one is maybe way down the list." And it's not as simple as it used to be. Back in the '80s, if you wanted to be a visionary business, all you had to do was say that you were going to incorporate computers—and you were an innovative business. Right now, multitudes of choice actually get in the way of people knowing what's a clear-cut path forward.

With so many technologies and innovations available nowadays, it can be overwhelming to know what to implement in your business. But do you know what your priorities are? When you know what your priorities are, you can make better choices to help your business.

Once you've implemented these secret weapons, what should you do?

Organizing your data is critically important. In all industries, data keeps coming up over and over again, and prioritization of that data is a really important part of it. Think about how you can pull information from different applications to get an insight that somebody else may not have. This will be really helpful in making you competitive in the market.

No matter what business you are in, you most likely have access to data. Whether it is sales and cost, analytics for advertising conversion, or more complex pieces of information, have you taken a good look at it to know how your business is performing? And have you used this information to make plans for your business down the road?

Three Action Steps

1. Identify technology and innovations that are good for *your* business. Cast aside those that are not going to help you move forward.

2. Prioritize your business needs and then use the innovations and technology that are going to move your business forward.

3. Analyze the data you have available to you and use that data to help you to prioritize and strategize your business's specific needs.

Connect with Scot at www.linkedin.com/in/mactaggart/

Opportunities Exist Everywhere

Ben Chai
Expert Strategist
Propertunities, Incoming Thought Limited

Ben works with 30-year-old entrepreneurs who want to achieve financial freedom. He helps people gain a roadmap on how to make their dreams become a reality. The roadmap is based on their dream life, their personality, their skill set, the time they have available, their connections, and creation of multiple income streams.

Main Takeaway

Opportunities exist wherever there are problems to solve.

Questions

1. There's been so much turbulence in markets across the globe. How can you create financial freedom even in this climate?

2. What is the difference between a lifestyle business and a corporate business?

3. What is the value of reaching seven figures in business?

4. How do you protect yourself and others around you from your own self-sabotage as you're growing and trying to create this financial freedom?

Interview: What do businesses need to know right now about financial freedom?

Ben is amazing. If you go look at his LinkedIn profile, you'll just see all that he's accomplished. Right now, he's focusing on 30-year-old entrepreneurs who want to achieve financial freedom. And he helps them gain a roadmap on how to make their dreams become a reality, a roadmap that's based on their dream life, their personality, their skill set, and the time that they have available, which is perfect, because so often, we just grab roadmaps that are designed in books that are standard and not in alignment with what we're doing. But his unique process helps them really home in on what they do best and what they want. He also helps them leverage their connections and create multiple streams of income.

There's been so much turbulence in markets across the globe. How can you create financial freedom even in this climate?

So, in terms of financial freedom in this climate, there are actually a lot of opportunities, tons and tons of opportunities. For example, I've been given an air sanitizer recently. There is nothing like this device on this planet. It sanitizes the air around you from coronavirus. The global situation created an opportunity.

There is a handheld one. There are bigger boxes that can either sit in the corner of a classroom or in a reception area. People come in, and maybe they've forgotten their mask, and you've run out of masks to give them. I don't like to use the word sanitized because sanitization of the air means to make it smell nice in many countries. But this is essentially taking the particles the size of coronavirus out of the air around you.

The opportunities exist everywhere.

A friend of mine just got into selling masks. She's now sold several billion. She only sells 3M quality because it's much cheaper. A friend of mine in Dubai was saying how he buys a mask that is probably a couple of cents. A mask in the UK is 1P. He says 100 for a Pound. The quality may not wear the same as, for example, a branded quality, right? But they're doing well.

Remote working is a big, big problem. In the UK, we've had hospitals that have been hacked. Many, many industries have found remote work to be very efficient. People save on time traveling and all that great stuff. They don't have to pay the overheads of lighting. And at the moment we're going through a heatwave in the UK; it is literally boiling. And those companies don't have to pay for air conditioning. They can save money that way. But their remote workers have potential hacking attacks on their routers, and they're not as well-defended as say a corporate server or corporate workstations. There is an opportunity for tech companies to start securing the home environment for remote workers, especially the senior executives.

It seems as though the pathway to financial freedom is by looking for opportunities, or ways to create solutions to the challenges that exist. The solutions are just as abundant as the challenges.

What is the difference between a lifestyle business and a corporate business?

You're making money to create your dream life. And I think this is essential for every business. I've recently been asked to write an article on scaling your business. And I had to think about this, because I realized that some business owners want a lifestyle business. So essentially, their scaling means, "I want to make more money; but I actually, I don't want to have more people in the company. I just want to be so efficient and make a certain amount of money."

There are limits on what you can make without having teams of people. It is resource limits. You can automate a lot. But you need to know whether you want a lifestyle business or you want to have a long-term corporate business. I had a business partner who was no longer a business partner, who kept saying, "I want to scale and grow my business," and we grew it to 4,050 people. But essentially, behind the scenes, he was funding his kids' schooling, he was funding all his holidays, which is fine for a lifestyle business. But then don't kid yourself, because eventually the business will collapse, because all that spending is being diverted from the company.

I think business owners sometimes get into the trap of not understanding the value of bringing on a team as it relates to scalability. You are foregoing short-term goals and outcomes financially in order to leverage what you're doing, the people that you're working with, and in the end, grow.

What is the value of reaching seven figures in business?

At five to seven years in a business, if you have reached that mark, the ability to grow is exponential. There's this differentiation that happens when you're making it to seven figures, you can do the first couple 100,000 solo and then you need a team. Then you need scalable systems in order to get to that last stretch. That's what takes you from the seven-figure mark to the exponential growth mark.

When I made my first seven figures, it was hard, hard, hard. It took me 11 years to do. I realized I didn't want to stress. I didn't want to be back in hospital and having outages in my health. I've gone a little bit differently by having teams that make less money, but it goes much faster. They've been developing the systems, which you are absolutely right about. In the recent business, we've hit seven figures to be shared amongst the executive team. I don't get the million on my own. But it's been so much more pleasant. It's been friendly, and you're happy going out and celebrating wins. All focus again around what our ultimate outcome is for that business, whether it's to sell, whether it's to grow and scale for a little while, like an Amazon or Facebook, or whether it's your lifestyle business, you have to know what you're trying to do.

How do you protect yourself and others around you from your own self-sabotage as you're growing and trying to create this financial freedom?

I ask people to do a Myers Briggs test or a big five test or DISC test or an Enneagram; in fact, do all of them. But then cross-reference what all those labels are. I get people to do all of that and get those reports. And that way I can see where their strengths are and where they can maximize their strengths and monetizable strengths and where they are actually sabotaging themselves and it's causing them to lose money.

Three Action Steps

1. Look for problems to solve as there will be a business opportunity.

2. Decide what type of business you are building: lifestyle or corporate.

3. Take the tests to learn about your personal strengths and weaknesses.

Connect with Ben Chai at www.linkedin.com/in/chaiben/

Revenue Kung-Fu

Erik Luhrs
Founder
Revenue Kung-Fu

Erik Luhrs is known as the Bruce Lee of revenue generation and is the creator of Revenue Kung-Fu. He works with founders of SaaS, technical service, and expert consulting companies who want to generate far more profit while also enjoying far more purpose and potential from their business and their lives.

Main Takeaway

Now is the time to look at your business and decide if this is really what you want to be doing. Decide if this is a dream worth pursuing or one that needs to be let go.

Questions

1. Where did you come up with the idea of Revenue Kung-Fu?

2. What do you think is the biggest challenge facing businesses right now?

3. How do you tap into the self-awareness that comes from the exploration of your business journey?

Interview: What do businesses need to know right now about Revenue Kung-Fu?

Eric Luhrs is known as the leader of revenue generation. He's the creator of Revenue Kung-Fu. He works with founders of SAS technical service and expert consulting companies who want to generate far more profit while also enjoying far more purpose and potential from their business in their lives. This is very much in alignment with what we do here at Sappari Consulting, and Erik is sharing what businesses need to know about Revenue Kung-Fu.

Where did you come up with the idea of Revenue Kung-Fu?

I started 15 years ago as a business coach. I studied neuro-linguistic programming and wanted to bring that into the business world. So, I got into sales and developed the Guru Selling System—and then I wanted to make sales better. Next, I evolved the Subconscious Lead Generation method, and then I wanted to make lead gen even better. So, I evolved the Peerless Positioning method, and then I wanted to make positioning better. So, I moved into brand development.

Ultimately, I realized that a brand flows from a person. So, Revenue Kung-Fu is your personal journey to create more of you, so that you can create more revenue. For certain businesses that are driven by a person or a small group of people, there's a purpose or a mission or a beingness behind it.

Kung Fu doesn't actually mean kicking people; it's actually Cantonese for "a skill acquired through perseverance." Revenue Kung-Fu is actually a journey; your journey through yourself to free yourself and then to free your revenue.

What journeys have you found yourself on with your business? And what skills have you acquired through perseverance?

What do you think is the biggest challenge facing businesses right now?

What's happening or what has happened is that COVID first knocked all of the pieces off the chessboard and then threw the chessboard. Then it flipped the table and threw the chair, and then it slammed the door.

COVID literally leveled the playing field.

What's happening is that the people who started what I call a "me-too business," which is a business where perhaps the owner is not passionate about their business but got into it because it's what they studied in college or where they could see the money, and are now hurting.

They're hurting because there are other people out there who are beating them on price. And these "me-too" businesses are trying to hit the same marks by delivering the same message via the same mediums—and they can't make it.

The biggest problem is those people don't know how to respond right now. They're not rebounding quickly. And they're asking themselves, "Well, what do I do? What do I do?"

This is your chance to start over again. There's no going back. But you can move forward.

Now, you need to ask yourself, "Who's going to move forward?" That's a very big question. Which version of you is going to move forward? This is your chance for rebirth. Who are you going to be going forward? When I say these things, remember it's not about going and finding another $62 billion industry to jump into. It's time to ask: Were you happy? Are you happy? What kind of life do you want now? Would you be okay making less money upfront with the potential to make more because you're enjoying yourself and you're really freeing yourself?

There's a chance for people now who have a real purpose and a real mission. For those who have a dream, or had a dream, and you want to bring it back together, this is the time to do it.

Why did you start your business? Was it because it was easy? Seemed like a quick way to make money? Or do you truly have a passion for it? Are you happy? These are hard questions to ask, especially if you don't think you'll like the answers. But use this time as an opportunity to explore your dreams.

How do you tap into the self-awareness that comes from the exploration of your business journey?

The first thing is to become aware of what was your dream, and where did it go off track? Did you have a dream? Did you leave a dream behind? Can you look at the different versions of your dream or the different things you've done and see a common theme? Can you see what you were after? And what can be a version of that going forward that can bring you fulfillment?

And there are many additional steps you can take but start there.

Lawrence Bossidy said, "Self-awareness gives you the capacity to learn from your mistakes as well as your successes. It enables you to keep growing." Have you tapped into it and used it to learn and grow?

Three Action Steps

1. Ask yourself how you see your business moving forward after COVID.

2. Use this as an opportunity to start over if you need to and develop a real purpose and mission for your business.

3. Reflect on your dreams and learn from them to move yourself and your business forward to find fulfillment.

Connect with Erik Luhrs at www.linkedin.com/in/erikluhrs/ or www.erikluhrs.com

Adaptation in Delivering Medicine

Dr. Ernesto Gutierrez
Physician & Entrepreneur
Practice Growth Formula

Dr. E is a physician who helps physicians. He coaches doctors in business and entrepreneurship. He believes that physician entrepreneurship, returning the business of healthcare to those who care for patients, is the way to fix the health crisis.

Main Takeaway

The pandemic has acted as a catalyst for medical technologies and physician care that will dramatically change within the next few years.

Questions

1. How long do you think things are going to take to go back to normal for doctors' practices?

2. What adaptations and adjustments do doctors need to be making now?

3. What do you recommend physicians do to stay ahead of the pack?

Interview: What do physicians need to know right now?

The pandemic of 2020 has been like nothing we've ever experienced, but for healthcare professionals, it's been challenging beyond words. Dr. Ernesto Gutierrez, known as Dr. E, is a physician who helps physicians. Dr. E. coaches doctors in business and entrepreneurship. He believes that physician entrepreneurship, returning the business of healthcare to those who care for patients, is the way to fix the health crisis. Dr. E wants to share what physicians need to know right now.

How long do you think things are going to take to go back to normal for doctors' practices?

The most important thing to understand right now is that this pandemic has acted as a catalyst. We're going to look back at this, and we're going to remember how things were before COVID and after COVID. And there's going to be a very clear distinction between the before and the after.

I don't think we're ever going back to "normal." We will eventually be developing a "new normal" that we will get used to. But things won't go back to being the same.

Think about 9/11, for instance. We never went back to how things were before, in terms of travel, for example. Now we have all these new security measures that we've gotten used to over the last 20 years. But these didn't exist before, and it's going to be very similar after the pandemic.

There are lots of doctors who are just waiting to weather the storm and then hoping that things will go back to normal. But this will not be the case. They need to be making changes in their practices, and it goes beyond just offering zoom video consultations.

As a physician, where are you on the continuum of wanting things to go back to "normal" or preparing for a "new normal" and making adjustments to the way you serve your patients?

John F. Kennedy once said, "Change is the law of life. And those who look only to the past or present are certain to miss the future." You don't want to miss the future.

What adaptations and adjustments do doctors need to be making now?

Small family practices are the ones that are better suited to pivot right now. It's a lot easier for them to implement big changes and start adapting.

For example, when people think about telehealth, they may think that it is just okay. Physicians worry that they won't be able to provide all of their services via telehealth. But the thing that we need to be mindful of is that this is just the beginning.

The pandemic has been the catalyst to have a lot of regulations that were in place removed. A lot of red tape has been removed, and this is going to open the door for a lot of new devices and technologies.

For example, we're going to start seeing remote diagnostic devices that people will either have at home or that will be able to be deployed to their homes. If you have a sick child, you may not have the time or want to take your sick child to a doctor's office filled with other sick children. So, wouldn't it be great if you had a device that could either plug into your phone or that you could have at home that will give your doctor real-time clinical data? Your doctor could receive all of your child's pertinent data and make a diagnosis and prescribe a treatment.

Technologies such as this will be coming. And physicians need to be prepared to start leveraging this technology.

Technology is advancing at a much more rapid pace. The innovations that we're going to see in the next two years are going to be much more than the ones we saw in the last twenty years.

Technology is supposed to solve the problems of time, energy, space, or matter. While technological changes for physicians may have been slow and steady for the last 20 years, rapid changes are coming, and now is the time to embrace those changes. After all, what could be better than improving the health of your patients?

What do you recommend physicians do to stay ahead of the pack?

While you really cannot know the specific direction that things are going, we are recommending that physicians start creating their own personal brand. They want to begin educating patients and potential patients because once new technologies become available, you're going to open yourself up to world-wide exposure.

New technologies will have doctors not only competing with physicians in their zip codes but with doctors across the country. The doctors in practices right now that are making the effort to build a solid, personal brand or a practice brand, that are educating people, and that are bringing value to them, despite them not being their patients right now—those are the doctors that are ahead of the pack. They will be in a better position to compete with the rest.

Do you have a brand? Does your practice have a brand? Have you ever even thought about your career as needing a brand? Creating a brand strategy now will make you stand out amongst your competitors in the future.

Three Action Steps

1. Prepare to start making changes in your practice because things are not going to go back to "normal."

2. Start leveraging new technologies as they become available.

3. Create a brand for you and your practice and begin educating and bringing value to your patients and potential patients.

Connect with Dr. E at www.linkedin.com/in/drernestomd/ and pgformula.com/

SALES

Prepare for All Seasons | 44
with Caitlin Doemner

Start & Continue the Conversation | 49
with Cat Stancik

Don't Stop Selling | 54
with Jeff Pugel

Create Your Conversion Equation | 58
with Terri Levine

SALES

How you sell matters. What your process is matters. But how your customers feel when they engage with you matters more.
—Tiffani Bova

For some businesses, like those in the travel industry, sales came to a complete standstill, and for others, like those in logistics and masks, sales skyrocketed. But for everyone, there was a question of what is the proper way to sell during a global pandemic. Without sales, our businesses do not exist.

Caitlin Doemner of BookofExperts.com was the first interviewee to delve into what businesses need to do to reopen. She shares the seasonality of business and what to do during each season. Number one rule to remember: always be conversing with your prospects.

Cat Stancik of Action Incubator tackles whether it is ethical to continue to sell when times are difficult. Her perspective? Know what problem you solve and be of service.

Jeff Pugel of Ignition digs into the biggest mistake that businesses make in times of crisis. He shares how to evaluate where you are in your business and whether or not to continue outreach. Adaptation and empathy are key components.

Terri Levine of Heartrepreneur LLC maps out the formula to solve the problem of prospects. Her four-step Conversion Equation teaches you how to reverse the marketing energy in your business and attract sales to you.

Prepare for All Seasons

Caitlin Doemner
Founder
BookofExperts.com

Caitlin, founder of Book of Experts, helps coaches and consultants significantly scale high-ticket offers by matching them with business development reps that align with their brand.

Main Takeaway

When the entire world stops, you have an opportunity to create the business you desire if you listen, plan, and change.

Questions

1. What are smart companies doing to prepare to reopen?
2. What will be different in the sales world now?
3. What's the missing piece?

Interview: What do businesses need to know right now about sales and getting back to work?

Caitlin Doemner of Book of Experts was interviewed April 28, 2020 for an article in Forbes entitled, "How smart companies are preparing to reopen."

We build sales systems that include three things: a process, a technology, and a person. We create a customized process, put our clients into our technological matching tracking system, and place them with one of our certified sales pros. In the end, they have an entire system that gets them consistently generating predictable cash flow for their business.

Without sales, you don't have a business.

What are smart companies doing to prepare to reopen? Is it time to move forward?

Yes, it's time to move forward. People are actively buying right now. There's a lot of money that's available right now. There's a lot of easy credit that you can apply for, there are loans available, and people are actively investing. We are seeing that they're investing in educational programs and a lot of technology. As we start reopening the doors, both literally and in our minds and hearts figuratively, as we start stepping back into society, what we're going to see is a really strong desire to not let this happen again.

What I would suggest is saying in your marketing how you can help create more safety, more security, and more predictability. People are looking to have a firmer foundation. When there are boom years, it's harvest time. We tend to extend ourselves. We leverage ourselves. We buy a lot and put ourselves into jeopardy because there's a lot of money to be made. We are now in a winter season. I don't want to say it's a recession or anything like that, because that has negative connotations. I think it's just a natural contraction. You need spring, but you also need winter.

Business winter is a time for you to dig into your own roots. Look at ways you can start prioritizing cash reserves and profit margins. This is an ideal time to pivot. You are able to completely reinvent yourself right now.

If you did everything offline, now is an opportunity to offer online. As I argue in the Forbes article, how we buy, how we consume, how we work, and how we produce are going to be permanently changed by what we are going through. We've gotten a taste for convenience that we are not going to want to let go. We will see people realize, "I don't have to live in a downtown area," and/or "I don't have to commute two hours to work." "I can work from anywhere." We will have a massive shift into online production and consumption. Think about the implications of that. It will be critical for understanding how business and life will play out moving forward.

There are many implications. It's not just in what you're saying. It's not just who you could sell to, but it's how your workforce wants to show up and do the work for you. I've seen opportunities for certain businesses. Businesses who thought they'd never go online suddenly have an online presence. And now an enormous market has just opened up to them. They can open up their storefront again, and they have this ability to generate revenue outside of their local area. People reached the client-base locally and now they can reach globally. We live in Pennsylvania and signed up for music lessons with Rogers School of Music in Minnesota. As the receptionist signed us up, she had to consider the time difference, new zip codes, etc. These are challenges that are exciting to solve.

What does this mean in the sales world? How would these current events show up with making or closing a sale or growing a sales team? What's going to be new and different now?

Right now, you need to put your listening ears on. Even if you have a sales team, get back into the thick of things and start getting on your own sales conversations. Don't enter a sales conversation with a pre-arranged agenda. Go back to the drawing board. I joke that everybody, except Charmin, is having to reinvent their business model. You need to go deep. But, go deep in your why.

What is your mission? Ask, what's really important to your values? Connect with that. Become anchored in you. What I think we're going to see is that the people who were mission-focused are going to surge right now because they never lost momentum. They're committed to getting their mission out into the world; people who were just doing it because it was easy money, they shrank in March and April 2020. It will take them longer to rebuild momentum because of the picture that they generated. Always stay close to your mission.

What that translates to is listening to your tribe. Talk to real people: past clients or future prospects or your current clients. Listen to where they are and what they're looking for. Chances are that has changed. If you assume, "Everything's back up and I'm just gonna sell whatever I used to sell at the price tag I used to sell it for," you're going to be in for a shock. You'll see the effect in your conversion rates.

People are going to be looking for safety, for security, for predictability. Business and life are not going to be, "Open the doors and people will flood back in." So little time has passed and the entire world has changed.

What's the missing piece?

The biggest thing is whether you've done online outreach or not; now is a great time to do it. This is what we specialize in at our company and we are seeing it boom more than ever. People are on social media. Even if they weren't active before this, they are now. This is a great place to engage with them and find prospects. We advocate a multiple channel approach. We focus on business to business (B2B). Business to consumer (B2C) is a little bit different.

Having real conversations with real human beings is always going to be your go-to. Learn how to find your ideal clients online. Start a real conversation with genuine curiosity. And then be prepared to love and serve them. Sales are all about love and service. And if you show up, ready to love and serve people, you'll win 100 percent of the time.

There is an uptick in people being on, available, and ready for a conversation. It's not true that you cannot do business in a crisis. People may be overwhelmed or not ready to buy yet. But there are myths to confront. It's important to listen and look for opportunities to move forward.

Three Action Steps

1. Prepare for a business winter even during times of growth. Consider opportunities that are created when you are forced to stop doing things the way you have always done them.

2. Listen to your customers by getting back into the conversation. If you have a sales team, jump back into doing the sales yourself so you have an understanding of what is going on.

3. Get online and start the conversation with your prospects. They are there and ready to engage.

Connect with Caitlin Doemner at
www.linkedin.com/in/cscdoemner/ or BookofExperts.com to talk about the sales process in your business.

Start & Continue the Conversation

Cat Stancik
Lead Boss
Action Incubator

The Founder of Action Incubator, bestselling author of *7 Principles for a More Productive and Fulfilling Life*, and creator of the Lead Boss System, Cat doesn't mess around when it comes to revenues or wasting time. Entrepreneur coaches, consultants, and service providers turn to her when they're ready to say *No* to time-consuming, overly automated, bro-marketing, shake-you-down gimmicks that leave everyone feeling less-than. Instead, they're ready to say *Yes* to a simple and strategic approach that saves them time, uses their unique voice, passion, and expertise, and turns their efforts into a consistent, predictable, organic lead gen machine. They'll use her process on *any* platform to hit their big revenue goals, so they can increase their impact *and* the amount of time they spend with their family.

Main Takeaway
Go back to what works and create a relationship.

Questions

1. What do businesses need to know right now about revenue and lead generation?
2. What about funnels and current strategies?
3. Are people buying? Is it ethical to sell something?
4. What would you tell someone connecting for the first time with social media?

Interview: What do businesses need to know right now about revenue and lead generation?

People have learned to market and to sell a certain way. And really right now, especially with what's going on in this current environment, people need to unlearn that. They need to go back to the things that have always worked. Whenever any kind of environmental catastrophic event happens, it's back to the basics of building the relationship. Talking to someone is always what converts. I know, it's not mind-blowing.

I'm gonna shake things up. It's not the technology. It's not the tool. It's you. Right? Most of the people that I work with— they are still their business. Whether they have employees or not, they are still the front of their business or the face of it. They need to build the relationships or put the processing systems in place to be able to do that. It's still about you. It's about your word, and how you show up. It's your values and finding people that align to that and doing it faster. It's about the quality over the quantity.

If we get down to the bottom of it, we get opportunities like this pretty regularly. For instance, a big client leaves and suddenly you have to shift back to what works. If you change the focus of your business, if you go in a new direction, client-wise or with a new product, these are all really great opportunities to shift your perspective and to go back to what works. And what you're saying works is building relationships, but doing it quickly.

How do you feel about funnels and the current strategies?

You said a lot of this stuff doesn't work.

The thing is that people use technology as a reason to try to shortcut things. Technology isn't a shortcut; technology amplifies. Whatever you've got going on in your business, technology will amplify that. If you're not able to consistently close clients on a regular basis at a certain pace and insert your sales process, technology isn't going to make that anything else, but will amplify what's going on right now. If you don't know how to talk to your clients, if you don't know how to convert, if you don't know how to overcome objections, technology isn't going to be able to do that for you, because you're going to be feeding the words to the technology. You've got to understand your client better than they even sometimes understand themselves. And you do that through practice.

Every single person that you've bought a high-value item from, you've talked to someone on the phone. You haven't just handed over $20,000 on your credit card through an application programming interface (API) system without actually engaging with someone. People are trying to hide from the thing that they're insecure about. If you're insecure about talking to people, and you're trying to hide behind the technology, it's not going to work for you. You've got to get the foundational components. You're in business, that means you're in the business of selling and marketing.

I hear a lot of people say, "I'm just going to do Facebook ads," or "I'm going to do Google Ads," "I'm going to pay for the different subscriptions that are available." That is an expensive experiment when you don't know how to get somebody from the "I'm thinking about buying from you" to the "I just bought something from you" stage. These things make sense to have as an automated system to go through the steps we are talking about. But, when what you sell is thousands of dollars and up, I have seen people hide behind technology, afraid to get out there. I don't want to be seen. They are afraid to be seen as the expert. Hiding behind technology will not help you close more sales.

You check the box of posting an image, creating a graphic

design, etc. It helps satisfy an egotistical component of you wanting to feel productive, but not actually being productive. What a lot of people don't understand is those funnels are called self-liquidating funnels, meaning they're not actually creating a profit. What they're doing is creating buyers to upsell. Why not go there faster and just upsell them with the higher ticket offer in the first place? Instead of adding barriers between you in the ask, which is what technology sometimes does. I'm not saying it doesn't work, but unless you have hundreds of thousands of dollars to put into a self-liquidating funnel to test and modify, you might as well make hundreds of thousands of dollars in your business by having the conversation.

Are people buying? Is it ethical to sell something?

People are buying, everyone's buying. Just because the tide is out doesn't mean that there's less water in the ocean. You've got to change how you're talking about what you do.

When it comes down to business, you have to ask, "What problem am I solving?" Right now the problems have shifted. Are you solving a problem that doesn't really exist anymore? Or have you modified how you talk about what you do, still using the same process to solve a different problem? It's all about what people are looking for. You have to sell them what they want. You can't make them want to buy what they need.

They don't want to buy what they need. No one wants to buy their vegetables, but they're going to buy the dessert that happens to come with a side of vegetables, protein, and starch. The dessert, that's what they want. If they're gluten-intolerant, then sell the gluten-free version of the dessert.

People are looking for something. And it's up to you to have the conversation and allow them to tell you what they want to buy. But so many times people get so caught up in their own process, themselves, and making business about themselves and trying to sell, instead of trying to figure out if it's a fit.

Any tips or advice on having that conversation if you're feeling reluctant, and you don't know where to start?

When you ask, "How can I help you?" the customer is thinking,

"You don't even know me." I appreciate the question of "How can you help me," but until we have a conversation, and we get to know each other, it actually may be me helping you or a recommendation to something else entirely.

I've seen a lot of people hopping on LinkedIn right now and I'm loving it. I love that people are getting really engaged in social media, but they could find some bad practices out there. What's the first step if you're just jumping into social media, or if maybe it's a platform you haven't used before?

What would you recommend for somebody to just connect for that first time with social media?

First of all, LinkedIn isn't meant for selling. So don't sell. Don't be "Pitchy Pete." We have all met him. He basically goes right from a place of pitch up, connect, and we'll tell you right off the bat, don't be him. I want you to go out and start a conversation, see how you can add value to that person. The entire foundational pillar of everything that I do is from a place of service first. When you take that approach, then you can receive more in terms of abundance.

Three Action Steps

1. Unlearn the current popular strategies and go back to what you know works.

2. Use technology judiciously once you have a process that works in order to amplify it.

3. Sell people what they want.

Connect with Cat Stancik at ActionIncubator.com/Jumpstart
Quickly activate the leads that are already around you and get people who are ready to pop their hands up to buy.

Don't Stop Selling

Jeff Pugel
CEO & Founder
Ignition

Jeff Pugel helps founders and sales teams scale their lead pipelines through the Opportunity Creation Process. By working within the Opportunity Creation Process—a B2B outbound marketing framework designed to stand out, build trust, and generate new revenue (without spamming inboxes and hiring someone that doesn't understand the professional services industry)—he and his team at Ignition take the pivotal task of prospecting and manage it for their clients until a lead raises their hand, allowing them to focus on running their business and selling, not prospecting.

Main Takeaway

Don't stop selling during difficult times. Now is the time to adapt or pivot to meet the needs of your customers.

Questions

1. What's the biggest sales mistake most small businesses make during downturns like this?

2. Why is it that businesses find themselves stopping

or pausing sales conversations during business downturns?

3 What are some easy things they can do to get out of this situation where the sales conversations have slowed or stopped?

Interview: What do businesses need to know right now about lead generation and sales?

What you need to know right now about lead generation and the nuance that needs to be brought to this topic at this time is something that needs to be discussed during these trying times. Jeff and his team take the pivotal task of prospecting and manage it for their clients until a lead raises their hand and says they're ready to move forward, at which point the process gets handed over. This can be a challenging thing, especially for business owners who love what they do. But going out and finding the clients can be really daunting.

The biggest issue most businesses have is working on the business versus working in the business. There are not enough hours in the day. As a business owner, you have 24 hours a day and 48 hours worth of stuff to do.

What's the biggest sales mistake most small businesses make during downturns like this?

The biggest thing is that they stop selling because they assume no one's buying.

Let's put some context here. It makes sense for certain businesses right now to stop. For example, if you're in the travel industry. It makes complete sense.

Yet, others are doing more business than ever.

I like to look at things in terms of stoplights. Your business is a red light, green light, or yellow light for sales at the moment. For those who may be in that yellow light zone, you don't stop the outreach right now. You need to change your look and keep the process going. You may need to adapt the messaging for the time being. That's probably the biggest change, realizing every-one's gone from "buy now" to "buy, but not right now."

How can you apply this stoplight metaphor to your business in the moment? Are you currently a red light, yellow light, or green light for sales? If you're a yellow light or green light, how are you adapting your sales messaging to meet your customers? And if you find you're a red light right now, what are you doing to lay the foundation to ensure your business continues to be viable going forward?

Why is it that businesses find themselves stopping or pausing sales conversations during business downturns?

A big reason is a lot of businesses like certainty. And right now, there's not a lot of certainty. It comes back to the mindset of the individuals who run those businesses. The biggest thing is mindset.

When it comes to being successful in business, mindset plays a huge role. An optimistic mindset will set the stage for success—even in difficult times.

What are some easy things they can do to get out of this situation where the sales conversations have slowed or stopped?

The biggest thing you can do if you've slammed on the brakes is just to get the machine moving again. Take a look at your current sales pipeline and figure out what your customers need. Find yourself an "easy win" right now by realizing everyone's needs have changed. For example, you may not be able to sell that $10,000 a month project now, but you may be able to sell a lot of $1,000 per month projects. Look within your offerings and adapt them based on the current environment.

Getting yourself a "win" by looking at what your current customers need in these challenging times can go a long way toward changing your mindset.

Winston Churchill shared this motto, "When you're going through hell, keep going." So, that's what I'm telling everybody.

That's what I'm doing, and you should be doing it too. Just keep walking.

Businesses are learning to pivot. When a downturn happens, new markets are being created to replace markets that have dried up. People are looking for new opportunities. A great example is gym owners. Many are shut down right now, but many have moved to online classes and are creating a huge library. Down the road, the online classes that have been created will be able to be monetized. They've adapted to the times and created a future potential opportunity.

Finally, approach everything with empathy. You don't know what's happening with that person you are trying to connect with. They may be fine, or they may have a spouse or a loved one in the hospital with COVID-19 at the moment. You just don't know. So, approach everything with a lot more empathy than you normally would.

Three Action Steps

1. Don't assume no one is buying and that you need to stop selling. Continue your sales conversations.

2. Adapt your offerings to meet the current needs of your customers and pivot, if necessary, to find new offerings that meet their wants and needs.

3. Approach everything with empathy—especially sales. You don't know what your customers are experiencing at the moment.

Connect with Jeff Pugel at www.linkedin.com/in/jeffreypugel

Create Your
Conversion Equation

Terri Levine
Chief Heart-repreneur®
Heartrepreneur LLC

Terri Levine is one of the world's top business strategists with proven methods for boosting small business fast. Her programs range from business coaching, consulting, and training to develop leadership skills, to creating professional training courses for others in the field of business coaching, and providing additional products and services to companies seeking support to become Heart-repreneur-based businesses.

Terri works with business owners to help them get an avalanche of qualified leads, close more sales, and make 200 percent ROI guaranteed.

Main Takeaway

By using the four steps of the Conversion Equation (interrupt, educate, engage, and offer), you can convert prospects into clients.

Questions

1. What is the biggest challenge businesses are facing right now?

2. What is the conversion equation?

3. Can you rely on referrals as a marketing strategy?

Interview: What do businesses need to know right now about business building?

Terri Levine has been in business for 43 years. She has had eight multimillion dollar businesses in all different kinds of industries. She's helped over 6,000 clients have the same kind of success in over 444 different industries. And she's sharing what businesses need to know right now about business building.

What is the biggest challenge businesses are facing right now?

Ever since the pandemic started, we've been contacted by over 600 businesses around the world, all asking for help. They don't have enough prospects, they're not closing enough sales. And quite frankly, they don't have the wealth that they need, sometimes even to keep their doors open. And many of them have to change their models, they may have to do something different. The number one thing that they're all afraid of is going out of business. And if they don't have more prospects, they will. So that's the one issue that I really want to help people with.

I don't think the prospects have gone anywhere; it is a matter of connecting. Your book is called The Conversion Equation.

What is the Conversion Equation?

You're right, the prospects are there and nothing's changed. I was looking back at my businesses over the years, and they all follow this formula called conversion equation, which is why they all really went from zero to hundreds of thousands of dollars, in one case, millions in a couple of months. The formula conversion equation has four parts.

> **Interrupt:** The first part is that you must have a message that interrupts your target audience. They're

busy, they're not really consciously paying attention. Unless your message interrupts them and gets them to go, "Now what is that?" they're going to miss it.

Engage: After you interrupt them, you must keep them engaged. If you don't have something engaging to say, then they're right back to scrolling or whatever they're doing.

Educate: The third part is you must educate them. Create value and educate them. Don't go right into some pitch or try to get them on your list.

Offer: The fourth step is offer. The offer needs to be a low-risk, no-cost offer. And I see way too often people are trying to sell the seven dollar item or this nine dollar offer. They don't begin a relationship with people. That is what the word heart-repreneur stands for. Stop transactions and do Heart to Heart marketing.

There is a shift back to a relationship building and conversation. Not just showing up and being flashy and disappearing.

Having a message that interrupts—I think a lot of people get that. They see ads, they see crazy pictures of the guy with the fancy car. If you want to market to women, all you need to do is show her relaxing in a bathtub because women don't want the fancy car.

Engage, have the conversation, educate, and then make an offer. Businesses may be following this process, but not actually making the offer. They're educating, but not taking them to the next step. I could see where there might be a challenge at each one of these steps. Decide which step you need to target.

Are there any businesses that are doing this really well?

I have a young gal named Jackie that came to me pretty much right out of college, and she didn't have any audience. She wasn't making any money. However, she had a really clever concept about helping people with Instagram where she grew a following. She just had nothing to sell them. And so we focused on getting a specific audience: young people your age who want to start a business and how to do it on Instagram. We came up with her four pieces of the conversion equation. We also created a high-ticket offer. Within six weeks she had $68,000 in revenue. Zero to sixty within a couple of months. After that, she was like $180,000. She did so well that she purchased a house, planned her honeymoon, and planned an extraordinary vacation. She's doing what she loves. She's serving people. She used the conversion equation which she wasn't using before.

If you have something that you know how to do really well, in her case Instagram, then the high-ticket offer is the way to go. Businesses make this mistake all the time, to focus on the low-ticket, low-value offer. You need to sell a lot. If you're selling $10 items, you need to sell 18,000 of those items to reach the target of $180,000 that Jackie reached. Focusing on that high-ticket, high-value offer that can really make a huge difference in how quickly you have success.

What is reverse marketing?

Most business owners spend all day hunting for leads on social media. Instead, we make a compelling offer following the conversion equation. You have to use all the pieces. Reverse marketing happens every day as people raise their hand. Today so far, we have 18 prospects. They raise their hands and ask for help. That's how I recommend you do business through reverse marketing, through standing out in your marketplace.

A lot of people say, "I don't have a marketing strategy," and they just do business by referral. So what do you say to those businesses?

That is the worst business strategy ever. And I can point to over 200 people who have said that over the years, and at some point went out of business. That is not a marketing strategy. And so you need to really get smart and you need to develop a marketing strategy. Remember, A-B-M, "always be marketing."

Do you need all four pieces of the Conversion Equation together before you can start?

You need all four pieces together and you need to do them

correctly. But then it works every single time if you do it correctly. The book, *The Conversion Equation*, goes through all of these steps in detail. And it has case studies in almost every different industry. So when you get the book, it also comes with massive bonuses. You invest $20 in a book and it's a tax write-off as it all goes to a charity foundation. Then you follow the equation. I literally take you by the hand and there's case study after case study where you will find people just like you, and the book is available right now.

Three Action Steps

1. Understand the number one challenge in business is finding prospects.

2. Implement the four steps of the conversion equation: interrupt, engage, educate, offer.

3. Always be marketing.

Connect with Terri Levine at www.linkedin.com/in/terrilevine/ and www.publishizer.com/conversion-equation

LEADERSHIP

Spiritual Leadership | 67
with Dana Moore

Leadership Can (and Should) Be Taught | 72
with Vanessa Judelman

Engage in Transparency to Create True Partnership | 77
with Skip Weisman

Conscious Leadership | 83
with Candice Kingston

LEADERSHIP

*The most dangerous leadership myth is that leaders are born—
that there is a genetic factor for leadership. That's nonsense; in
fact, the opposite is true. Leaders are made rather than born.*
—Warren Bennis

Many leaders were made in the crucible of this pandemic. As a business owner, you lead your employees and customers, too; they look to you for guidance as a leader. Social media amplifies what you do as an authority. What is needed in the leadership space right now? These four interviews answer that question as we tackle the need for leadership in crisis. Bottom line is that what makes you a great leader is you being more *you!*

Dana Moore of Inspired Lightwork, LLC guides us to tap into our inner goddess to be the leaders the world needs right now. We do this by connecting intuition and spiritual texts, using personal energy management practices (PEMP), and understanding that spirituality and business are not two separate entities.

Vanessa Judelman of Mosaic People Development has a strong, clear message, "Leadership can be taught." All businesses need a leadership development strategy, and they need to practice leadership as part of their routine.

Skip Weisman of Your Championship Company brings his skill set as a former professional baseball CEO to the business world. His leadership principle? Workplace transparency that empowers everyone in the company with knowledge.

Candice Kingston of Kingston Coaching encourages us to use conscious leadership to bring our whole selves into our leadership roles, embrace our human experience, and have empathy.

Spiritual Leadership

Dana Moore
Founder & Spiritual Director
Inspired Light, LLC

Dana N. Moore, founder of Inspired Lightwork, LLC, helps passionate women business owners lean into their leadership potential to achieve the next level of their business and life. Dana has operated her virtual business for over 10 years with a broad range of certifications in operational services and technology, as well as therapeutic and spiritual studies. Through a unique combination of teaching Personal Energy Management Practices (PEMP) and providing traditional strategic planning services and operational oversight, Dana helps her clients achieve greater clarity in pursuit of their personal and business goals and the confidence to *go for it*!

Main Takeaway

Adding a spiritual practice to your day can help you to lead with clarity, confidence, and compassion.

Questions

1. What's something you do each morning to start your day?

2. What do you do with your clients to assist them

spiritually?

3. As a leader in your business or as a leader in your community, how can you infuse more clarity, confidence, and compassion into your work?

Interview: What do businesses owners need to know right now about tapping into their inner goddess to be the leader the world needs?

Dana Moore wants women entrepreneurs to activate their inner goddess and to show up powerfully in business and in leadership. She helps spiritual entrepreneurs step into their divine calling to lead, which often shows up as a divine mission. Dana's skills make her the ideal person to share what businesses need to know right now about tapping into your inner goddess to be the leader the world needs.

What's something you do each morning to start your day?

One of my personal practices is pulling a card, pulling the guidance card every morning. Some people call this divination, and some people use this as a spiritual practice. You may be familiar with it, for example, with tarot cards or Oracle cards, or even something as simple as flipping through the Bible or other religious texts and letting your eyes, mind, and spirit guide you to the message that you need for that moment in that day.

I've learned to do it in my various studies of world religion. It is grounding, and it honors the divine feminine power that flows through all of us. All of us are born through a woman. We are all attached to that energy. And that doesn't mean that we don't need the masculine and honor the masculine and love the masculine. But women's energy is about change and really touching and creating a wall. Right now, we need to know that there's a lot of change going on in the world and that we are also called to change in many ways. We won't provide if we try to continue to do things in the same way, and we're seeing that right now.

And so, I like to call on the goddesses using the Goddess

Guidance Oracle deck. I'm just going to pull a card for us. What do we, as business owners, business leaders, and spiritual leaders, need to know right now? What comes up is Brigit. She says, don't back down; stand up for what you believe is right.

Do you have a morning routine? Something you do to start your day off right? What does it look like for you?

What do you do with your clients to assist them spiritually?

In my work, I guide my clients, my friends, and my loved ones to be connected to that inner voice and their core values. We find that those who are most successful, as Brendon Burchard mentions in his book *High Performance Habits*, are business owners and leaders who have a routine. They have a nonnegotiable practice. And much of that includes a spiritual practice.

Spiritual practices can look like prayers, journaling, and writing, even exercising. It's really what connects you to a sense of being grounded and having clarity and confidence. Spiritual practices and the way that we are gentle and compassionate with ourselves helps us to be gentler and more compassionate in the world. And again, it's what we need right now.

Do you have nonnegotiable practices that are part of your daily life? What are they—and why are they nonnegotiable for you? Knowing "the why" helps you to make them a habit that brings success.

Our businesses are an outpouring of our own inner mission. Connecting the routine of spirituality into your business and leadership can help give you direction.

Conflict arises when our actions don't line up with our beliefs. And that causes conflict inside of us. As a global community, we're experiencing conflict, and our actions are not really lining up or aligning with what we desire to bring to our world, who we are, the kinds of communities that we've decided to create, and how we want to care for and love one another.

Many of us in business are entrepreneurs and business leaders because we have a mission. We have a desire to bring forth in the world something that's important, something that will make this world a better place, and we are called to do that work.

There are those who are feeling that pull inside, that feeling that there's something more they should be doing, or that maybe there's something they should be saying. You need to show up in the world and continue learning and discovering. This is a time of transition and transformation. Be gentle with yourself because you are being called. And it doesn't mean that you have to fight with yourself to get there. It means to pause, listen to deep within, and do the next right thing.

The spirit calls you to do, and you will continue to be supported. If you find that you're having trouble identifying that message or what your spirit is calling you to do, then it's time to institute a personal energy management practice or a spiritual practice.

I like to do that in very gentle ways. One thing that I love to share is a musical meditation that calls us to become gentle and compassionate with ourselves while opening us up to the messages of support, love, and action.

Clarity, confidence, and compassion are the qualities that business leaders need. Which of these three things are you excelling at right now? Is there one of these qualities where you need to put more of your focus and energy?

As a leader in your business, or as a leader in your community, how can you infuse more clarity, confidence, and compassion into your work?

Spiritual practice is important.

Confidence, at its origin in Latin, translates to *with faith*. And when you put them together, it doesn't necessarily mean that you're showing up strong and doing all the work; it means that you are moving with faith. Find your faith within—whatever that is for you—just find your faith. Listen to that small voice and move.

If you've felt disconnected from that side of yourself or want to activate it, now may be an ideal time to do so. Spirituality and business do not need to be two separate entities.

Three Action Steps

1. Start your day with a nonnegotiable practice that sets you up for success.

2. Lead with clarity, confidence, and compassion.

3. Find your faith and know that spirituality and business do not need to be two separate entities.

Connect with Dana Moore at
www.linkedin.com/in/dana-n-moore-b4930b172/ or
bit.ly/mygoddessactivation

Leadership Can (and Should) Be Taught

Vanessa Judelman
President
Mosaic People Development

In most organizations, people are promoted into leadership positions without any training. But being a leader and managing people has a unique set of skills. Vanessa Judelman teaches people those skills. She teaches them how to be self-aware and authentic as a leader. She teaches them how to build, develop, and coach a high-performing team. She teaches them how to lead their business strategically.

Main Takeaway

There are three pillars to learning to be a leader: know myself, manage my team, and lead my business—and these are skills specific to leadership that can be taught.

Questions

1. Why is it so difficult to transition into a leadership position?

2. How can people learn to be leaders? What does that

look like?

3. What are the most important key skills for leaders to develop first?

Interview: What do businesses need to know right now about leadership?

In most organizations, people are promoted into leadership without any training, but being a leader and managing people requires a very unique set of skills. Vanessa Judelman teaches people those skills. She teaches them how to be self-aware and authentic as a leader. She teaches them how to build, develop, and coach a high-performing team. She teaches them how to lead their business strategically. Vanessa is sharing what businesses need to know right now about leadership.

Why is it so difficult to transition into a leadership position?

Let's start with the age-old question: Are leaders born or made?

Leaders are definitely made. Some people are born with a certain amount of charisma and know-how to lead, but most leaders are made.

The problem is that in most organizations, people are promoted into leadership roles without education. And I always say, "Can you imagine if you had a teenager, and it was time for them to learn to drive. And you just said, 'Here are your car keys! Off you go and drive!'" You would never do that. It's the same with the leadership role.

Why do organizations promote people into leadership positions and then basically say, "Drive!"? Because most people learn to be an architect or an engineer, or whatever their skill set is when they're in college and university, and then go into the work world. They become an expert in that area and get promoted into leadership—because they're good at their job. But leading involves a completely separate set of skills.

In her book Mindset: The New Psychology of Success, *Carol Dweck wrote, "Growth mindset is based on the belief that your basic qualities are things you can cultivate through your efforts." And with this mindset, leaders can definitely be made.*

What does learning leadership look like?

Leadership is vast. It's complex. And the first thing that I do is always break down leadership into three pillars. I assess my clients against these three pillars and where they have gaps, we then focus on development.

The first pillar is **know myself**. Leaders must be self-aware.

The second pillar that's critical for leaders is **manage my team**. You have to know how to coach how to develop your people, how to give feedback, and have crucial conversations.

The third pillar is **lead my business**. Leaders have to know how to execute strategically. For example, a lot of leaders will say to me, "Vanessa, my boss has told me I need to be strategic, but I don't know what that means." So, that's an example of a skill that I teach people. I teach them that there are three parts of strategy. They learn exactly what it looks like to be strategic.

In that "lead my business" section, change management and leading change are skills that I teach my clients as well. All leaders have to lead and manage change, especially in today's environment. But they don't know that there are a set of skills and tools that you can leverage to communicate change and to bring people along in terms of changing their mindset, so they're more aligned when it comes to your change plan.

You have to give feedback, but a lot of times, people fear feedback because they don't know how to give it properly. But that's a skill that you can learn. There are tools associated with giving constructive feedback that leaders can learn and practice.

You practiced your skills for your designated profession over and over before you stepped into that role. But what about your leadership skills? How did you practice those skills? Or were you ever really taught them?

What are the most important key skills for leaders to develop first?

It's interesting that you mentioned growth mindset because I love the work of Carol Dweck. I am a huge fan. And she talks about fixing the growth mindset. So, I think a growth mindset and self-awareness are huge. That's the first step—because when you're in a fixed mindset, you believe everything is set in stone. Nothing can change. But when you're in a growth mindset, you know that with hard work, you can focus on anything and develop a new skill.

Leaders have to learn new skills every day. At this time, for example, leading virtually. Many of my clients have never done that before. That is a new skill.

I had a conversation with a client last week, and she said, "I have to give some negative feedback. Am I allowed to even do that in this stressful environment?"

I said, "Of course you are. I encourage it. Life goes on." Then she asked, "But how do I do that when I can't meet someone for coffee and do it face-to-face?"

So, the growth mindset is important. Feedback is important. And coaching is really important as well.

Coaching is a wonderful skill to have. The bottom line of coaching is really exceptional communication and listening skills—and those are definitely learnable. And some people may have some innate capabilities. But beyond that, you can learn great questions to ask, and you can learn to stop talking and be a good listener.

The reason I have these three pillars, know myself, manage my team, and lead my business, is so my clients are really clear on the core components of leadership, which is a very broad topic.

I have integrated these three pillars into an eight-module leadership program. I take leaders of all levels through this program to ensure that everybody understands the same tools and uses the same language across the organization. For example, there is an assessment tool that I love to use, and I highly recommend organizations assess all of their people. This allows people to understand their strengths and weaknesses. It also allows leaders to understand how best to coach and motivate their people.

I recommend that all organizations have a leadership development strategy in place. Having strong leaders in an organization is critical to moving any strategy forward.

It can take years to roll out a strategic leadership plan because there are so many components to it.

Many organizations have emergency plans, and everybody knows the protocol when there's an emergency. So, in the same way, what's the protocol for leadership?

Organizations that are doing leadership well have leaders who are self-aware. It means that their leaders know how to coach and develop their teams. It means that leaders really know how to take the vision of the organization, trickle it down, and hold people accountable.

Three Action Steps

1. Recognize that very few leaders are "born," but instead, they are "made" and can learn to be effective leaders.

2. Use the three pillars to become an effective leader: know myself, manage my team, and lead my business.

3. Know that the growth mindset is critical for becoming a leader. Try new skills. Don't worry if you fail initially. Keep practicing these skills until they become second nature.

Connect with Vanessa Judelman at
www.linkedin.com/in/vanessajudelman/ or
www.topleadershipskills.com

Engage in Transparency to Create True Partnership

Skip Weisman
Founder of Your Championship Company
Your Championship Company

Skip Weisman is a former professional baseball CEO who now works with business owners and CEOs to create championship company work environments (cultures) that are more positive, more productive, and even more profitable.

Over the last 18 years since leaving his baseball career, Skip has created powerful proprietary intellectual property to help leaders communicate and motivate employees across generations. In 2018, Skip published his first book, *Overcoming The 7 Deadliest Communication SINs: A New Standard for Workplace Communication.*

Main Takeaway

There are three areas of business that require transparency. You should be transparent with your company strategy, your performance expectations, and your financials.

Questions

1. What is workplace transparency?

2. Is there a line that you don't cross when you're being transparent?

3. Have you seen companies be more transparent in this current environment, or do you see them closing off?

Interview: What do businesses need to know right now about transparency?

Skip Weisman is a former professional baseball CEO who now works with business owners and CEOs to create championship company work environments (cultures) that are more positive, more productive, and even more profitable.

Over the last 18 years since leaving his baseball career, Skip has created powerful proprietary intellectual property to help leaders communicate and motivate employees across generations. In 2018, Skip published his first book, Overcoming The 7 Deadliest Communication SINs: A New Standard for Workplace Communication. *Skip is sharing what businesses need to know right now about transparency*

What is workplace transparency?

It's about having an open dialogue and communication in a work environment that really has gone missing, but it's never really been part of the work environment. It's always been the business owners who know what's going on. They know the financials. They know the numbers. They know the strategy and all that stuff. And the employees are just collecting a paycheck and doing their job. And those two things don't need to meet, right? The business owner just cracks the whip.

And so, especially as we head into the third decade of the 21st century, with the younger generation coming in, transparency is so important. And now we have the COVID-19 virus, and businesses are really struggling. But if a business really wants to stay relevant, then we need to start opening up our minds and the communication in a work environment and start bridging the gap—the communication gap, in addition to the generation gap.

And you do that by being more transparent. And you do that in three different ways.

There are three different concepts that I work on with my clients. One is the vision of strategy. What's your company about? Where are we going? A lot of times, the business owners don't share that for a lot of reasons, as they may not think the employee needs to know it, or they may think that they don't care. Or perhaps they've tried it before, and they got glazed-over eyes, and nobody does or says anything different. Or perhaps they don't even have a strategy—they haven't even thought about themselves.

And so, all of those reasons hold companies back because everybody wants everybody rowing in the same direction? So, it's a great metaphor.

The challenge is to do that, you have to have information, and you have to have knowledge.

People say knowledge is power. But a lot of times, business owners feel like too much knowledge gives the employees too much power. And that's going to cause problems.

The challenge is that knowledge is empowering. If you have the right knowledge, you can take action in that way. So, the first thing is that vision and strategy.

The second thing is in performance management and performance expectations. There are a lot of businesses that don't create clarity around performance expectations. What do I expect from you? What are the behaviors and performance results that you need to achieve in your role? And they hold on to it, or they don't think about it, or they don't like to have those difficult conversations about performance. And so, we don't have them.

On the flip side, there are two parts to performance feedback. The management and the leadership of the company have to be open to having that conversation to get feedback from employees. How am I doing? Like Mayor Koch in New York City in the '80s. He would go around town as mayor, asking people, "How is he doing? How am I doing?" Business leaders need to do that if they expect employees to be open to constructive feedback. They also need to be open to feedback as well and have that dialogue on performance. How are we doing in the work environment that makes that very transparent?

And then, the third level that gets a lot of business owners a little out of sorts is financial transparency. How are we doing financially? Are we making profits? Are we generating cash? What's the reality of our finances? And that gets a little dicey because people don't like to share the numbers and the money side of things. But without that, we have people who have entitlement mindsets, who expect that raise every year and the bonus at the end of the year all the time. They're very contentious conversations. Because the boys don't understand where the money comes from. And they think it's just falling from heaven. And the business owner is the only one worrying about it. So, when we open up the books, and we are transparent with the finances, employees get it, and they see what it takes to turn profits and where cash comes from. And they see whether there's money for bonuses or salary increases, and it just changes the conversation and the dynamic.

I've had many business owners come to me, and one of the things they say is, "I want my employees to take ownership of their jobs. I want them to be more proactive in their jobs and take ownership." Well, you take ownership when you have an idea of what that really means. You don't have to give equity in your company away. But trusting your employees enough to know the numbers and understand the numbers, and seeing how profit is made, helps people take accountability for their role in helping make that happen. If I'm just operating in the dark, I don't care what the materials to make that widget are, because it's not coming out of my pocket. I don't get it.

Have you shared your company strategy, your performance expectations, and your financials with your employees? What did you notice when doing that? Did you build trust? Achieve goals? Improve operations or profitability? All of these things—and more—can happen when you are transparent.

Is there a line that you don't cross when you're being transparent?

Yes, you have to be careful about that. But I think the pendulum needs to swing. And business financials can be very complicated, and a lot of companies are complicated.

So, we want to make it easy and simple enough for employees to understand and see the connection between what I do today and how that drives profits and generates cash for a company. And you can do it very simply. And it builds high levels of trust because employees feel like you're sharing this with me. Everybody's worried about, "Well, we're making more money, and employees are going to want more money . . ." Well, they already want more money, and those conversations are already contentious. And so now you can have a conversation about what's reality—what's real—and they can see where it comes from.

But on the flip side of that, we also add some accountability. You can't hide in a transparent work environment when you are a part of it—and a part of this is performance management. So, if we're going to trust you with the financials and knowing this stuff, then that comes with some responsibility and accountability. That means you're going to have to perform, and we'll have clear performance expectations. Those things work together to get everybody rowing in the same direction towards a much more profitable company, and it ends the entitlement mindset.

How comfortable are you with sharing the finances of your company? Did you see an improvement in employee performance, responsibility, and accountability when they became invested in the financial health of your business?

Have you seen companies be more transparent in this current environment, or do you see them closing off?

It depends.

Most small businesses are starting to have to be more transparent and open up because of the environment—especially around safety issues and what the protocols are and things like that. And this is going to add costs to a business, no doubt. So, the more expenses come on, if you really want your employees to buy into what you're doing, the best way to do it is to be more transparent. Be open and realize that you need them, and they need you, and it is a true partnership. And the more information everybody has, the more empowered they will be to act accordingly.

Remember that transparency can be empowering for everyone!

Three Action Steps

1. Be transparent with your company strategy, your performance expectations, and your financials.

2. Keep it simple when sharing your financials, but know that it's important for your employees to understand their impact on this part of the business.

3. Engage in transparency to create a true partnership between you and your employees.

Connect with Skip Weisman at www.linkedin.com/in/skipweisman/ or www.YourChampionshipCompany.com/pages/ycc/yeee/op to receive the "Employee Excuse Eliminator Checklist."

Conscious Leadership

Candice Kingston
Coach for small business owners and high-level professionals
Kingston Coaching

Candice Kingston works with small business owners and high-level professionals to help them grow personally and professionally. She uses energetic leadership coaching techniques to help uncover roadblocks that may be holding you back from reaching your true potential and creating a life and business you love. She spent 12 years in the corporate world (working in health insurance) not fitting in, and through the help of coaching, discovered a place where she finally felt like she could make an impact and help others.

Main Takeaway

Conscious leadership has you bringing your whole self to leadership. With conscious leadership, you have a strong self-awareness and use core values to lead in a responsive, not reactive, manner.

Questions

1. What is conscious leadership versus traditional leadership?

2. How can people apply conscious leadership to the

current situation?

3. How can we continue to be productive while working from home and putting conscious leadership into practice?

Interview: What do businesses need to know right now about leadership?

Candice Kingston works with small business owners and high-level professionals to help them grow personally and professionally. She uses energetic leadership coaching techniques to help uncover roadblocks that may be holding you back from reaching your true potential and creating a life and business that you love. She spent 12 years in a corporate environment—working in health insurance— but after realizing that it was not a fit, through the help of coaching, she discovered a place where she finally felt like she could make an impact. She's here to help us understand what businesses need to know right now about leadership.

What is conscious leadership versus traditional leadership?

Conscious leadership is about you bringing your full self—your whole self—to your leadership.

As a business owner, you don't want just the one piece of you that is a good leader. We want your full self—and in order to do that, you need to be conscious, which basically just means aware. Having a real solid self-awareness of who you are as a person, knowing your strengths, knowing your weaknesses, living your values, your priorities—all of that together brings your full self to that leadership role.

What we've seen as traditional leadership has been more reactive instead of responsive.

Conscious leadership relies on your values. Every decision should be coming from your core values and those of your company. By having a strong sense of those values and a sense of who you are—that self-awareness—you're going to be able to lead from that place and be responsive instead of reactive.

Do you know what your leadership style is? Are you more traditional and reactive in your response? Or have you adapted a conscious leadership style? If you still tend to be more traditional, do you know the core values that are important to you and your business? Can you use them to help lead?

How can people apply conscious leadership to the current situation?

At the end of the day, a conscious leader is looking at every problem as an opportunity, which can be tricky in a pandemic.

A pandemic offers a lot of problems/opportunities. When it comes to business decisions and having to pivot or change product offerings, look at this as a time of innovation. We have seen amazing things come out of this horrible crisis.

People have had to pivot. People have scrambled and put together things quickly, and this is happening because people are looking at it as an opportunity. This is one door that closed, but where's the door going to open?

That's really all it is. It's just shifting the lens that you're looking through. Instead of looking at it through a negative lens, think, "How can I shift things or make a change or start producing a different thing?"

The whole point of being a conscious leader is that you are leading with your whole self.

What lens are you looking through right now for your business? Are you focusing on the negative? Are you learning to see this as an opportunity to innovate? If you've moved to see this as an opportunity, how did you go about changing your mindset?

How can we continue to be productive while working from home and putting conscious leadership into practice?

It's really about embracing that human experience.

During this time, you need to be open to connecting with your employees. How can you share and show them what's happening with you? Can you say, "Wow, my kids are really struggling with this homeschooling thing. How are you guys doing? What's going on?"

We're in a new era of Zoom calls. By having more empathy

and more compassion as a leader—and starting with yourself and that self-awareness—then you can lead others.

Empathy and compassion are two important words during these times, but they're often not associated with business. Yet they're important traits for leaders to have. And while you probably have them, are you showing them? Or are you fearful about sharing these attributes? What's keeping you from sharing them?

Three Action Steps

1. Assess your leadership style to see if you are a conscious leader or a traditional leader. If you tend to lean towards traditional, determine how you can become a more conscious leader.

2. Change your lens to see problems as opportunities.

3. Be cognizant of showing your employees empathy and compassion as part of leadership.

Connect with Candice Kingston
at www.linkedin.com/in/kingstoncandice/
or www.Kingstoncoaching.com where you can
book a complimentary discovery call.

FINANCIAL

Create a Cash Flow Strategy | 91
with Camille Nisich

Integrating Business & Personal Finance | 95
with Jason Howell

Allow Your Agent to Be a Trusted Advisor | 100
with Kieffer Rittenhouse

Health Care Cost Containment | 105
with Allison De Paoli

Do Your Research on Tax Strategies | 109
with Murray Beaulieu

FINANCIAL

An investment in knowledge pays the best interest.
—Benjamin Franklin

An investment in financial knowledge doubles that interest. These next experts remind us that what businesses need to know right now is to have a financial plan that aligns with their business values.

Camille Nisich of Camille Nisich Consulting starts us off by focusing on a cash flow strategy. It is important not to stop the flow of money while still being mindful of your reserves. And invest time in innovative thinking so that you stay resilient.

Jason Howell of the Jason Howell Company encourages us to create a business with intention. Pay attention to both your numbers and be savvy with your knowledge of the legislation from your government that can affect your business.

Kieffer Rittenhouse of Integrated Insurance Solutions reminds us of the importance of tapping into expert advice. You want to keep your insurance provider aware of your changing situation because they can help you navigate those changes and make adjustments as needed, saving you money.

Allison De Paoli of Altiqe Consulting is on the cutting edge of healthcare insurance. What she says is to ask for the data about your claims. Your insurance coverage decisions should be based on the analysis of this data. In addition, there are nontraditional options that could be a better fit.

Murray Beaulieu of Boosted Profits brings his 35 years of experience as a controller/cost accounting manager to strategies for tax and expense savings. There are tax credits available to 90 percent off for businesses that they are not taking advantage of, and it's always prudent to look at your expenses. Now is the time to do something different to improve your company's financial situation.

Create a Cash Flow Strategy

Camille Nisich
Investor & Profitability Advisor
Camille Nisich Consulting

After earning her MBA and spending 18 years driving projects that turned Dell Technologies into what it is today, Camille Nisich helps fast-growing companies stop cash leakage, using big tech secrets, so they can quickly turn capital into profit. She has delivered over $100 million in savings and $1 billion in sales pipelines to help emerging companies grow.

Main Takeaway

Be smart about your cash flow reserves, but don't shut down your spending as it may impede you when you are ready to ramp back up.

Questions

1. What should businesses know about Paycheck Protection Program (PPP) Loan forgiveness?

2. How should business owners think about cash flow right now?

3. How can business owners create personal resilience, so it shows up in their business?

Interview: What do businesses need to know right now about cash flow strategies?

Camille Nisich is a cash flow strategist. Her consulting business helps female entrepreneurs create a cash flow strategy, gain access to funding, and design profitable businesses with her Resilience Reset Action Plan. She's here to share what businesses need to know right now about cash flow strategies.

What should businesses know about PPP Loan forgiveness?

About a week ago, there was a PPP deadline. And so, at the eleventh hour, there was an extension. It was originally June 30 for the approval, and it has now been extended to August 8. So, there's still time to get loans.

Some big banks that you can think of are not lending PPP anymore. However, there are still community lenders and small fintechs[1] that are. So even if you don't have a relationship with them, or maybe even you haven't heard from them, you can go one of two routes. You can either go to your larger lender and ask for a referral, or get creative, get online, and see what kind of lenders are still out there offering up PPP.

There was also a flexibility act, a PPP Flexibility Act, that was passed on June 5. And the requirements are looser in terms of how long the term of the loan is, how long the deferral period is, etc. So, it's actually a lot more accessible—even what you can do with the money changed. It used to be that you had to use 75 percent of it for payroll, and that's relaxed to 60 percent. So, there's still a huge opportunity there. It's just really important for people to know and understand that and to apply.

Even though there are some big banks that aren't offering these PPP loans anymore, there are still options out there. You need to look locally and ask questions to see what is available.

---

1 — According to Wikipedia, Fintech is the abbreviation of financial technology. Fintechs seek to compete with traditional financial methods and delivery of services and include services and technologies such as PayPal, Venmo, cryptocurrency.

I know that a lot of times, there was hesitation concerning, "Well, I'm not certain I'll be able to qualify for forgiveness; therefore, I'm not sure I want to even apply,"—and there is actually a provision for partial forgiveness. You might have forgiveness around the payroll piece, just as an example. Then if you have to repay, you still have a five-year loan term from the point of the designation on whether you get forgiveness or not. So, there is partial, and there's a five-year loan to loan term.

How should business owners think about cash flow right now?

The obvious thing is to be smart about your reserves. When you find yourself asking, "Well, do I have money? Have I been burning through it?"—and that's really important—you also need to not necessarily stop the flow.

The whole reason why things like stimulus packages exist is so that we don't stop the flow. Because when money is not flowing, it can't create more money. So, you just have to be really smart about your reserves. And that means having really deep, meaningful, even creative conversations with your partners, with the people in your supply chain, with your employees, and figuring out a solution that works for everybody.

Everybody is in a challenging position or has been affected, and people are willing to have conversations and to get creative and to share resources, but you need to have those conversations and think smartly about the reserves.

But don't stop spending. Again, it could get you into a risky situation in some cases, and it also can impede your ability to ramp back up.

If you are in a challenging position right now, it's worth reaching out to your vendors and providers. They may be able to help you bridge that gap, which is beneficial for everyone because if you stay in business, you remain a client, and that helps them stay in business as well.

I ask my clients, "What does your pivot look like?" And then I ask, "What do those relationships that are really critical to your business look like?" And I encourage them to go foster those. And that's even with your customers. Even if they are not buying from you, take the opportunity to get into a dialogue with them. Find out what they need and see what their challenges are. See what has best served them in the past and put that into your plan.

How can business owners create personal resilience, so it shows up in their business?

One of the things that I always talk about with my clients is, "What is your zone of genius time? And are you doing things in that zone of genius time for yourself?"

Typically, what happens is they say, "Oh, my zone of genius time is the morning. Well, I'm going to immediately get to work on my business. I'm going to send emails. I'm going to do all the things." But actually, that's the time where your innovative thinking comes in. So, make sure you have some personal habits that replenish you, that reboot you, that get you started, or wrap you up for the day. Then you can actually apply that into your business—into everything from how you get mental clarity or how you maintain your focus with all the different inputs that are coming at you. It might mean shutting some things off. It might mean putting your phone on "Do Not Disturb." But take some active role in your own habit-forming and your own kind of habit processes so that you can have that show up in your business.

Do you conscientiously set aside time for deep work? Are you using your zone of genius time for what you should be—innovative thinking?

Three Action Steps

1. Investigate all of your options regarding PPP loans— even if your regular lender is no longer participating.

2. Be smart about your cash reserves.

3. Know when your zone of genius is and use that time for innovative thinking.

Connect with Camille Nisich at www.camillenisich.com

Integrating Business & Personal Finance

Jason Howell
President/Family Wealth Advisor
Jason Howell Company

Jason Howell is a Certified Financial Planner professional, a former US congressional candidate, and in 2019 was listed as a top Wealth Advisor by Washingtonian magazine. He is president of the Jason Howell Company, a family wealth management firm that uses a sustainable, responsible and impact investing (SRI) discipline to develop parents into patriarchs and matriarchs of their communities and their families. His mission is to bring the best of the ultra-high net worth family's wealth management services to regular net worth families.

Main Takeaway

Creating a business with intention and knowing your financial numbers will help you achieve the goals that you set for yourself and your family.

Questions

1. What do people need to know about finance right now?

2. What do business owners need to know about finance right now?

3. Do you work with businesses to help bring these concepts and ideas to their employees as well?

Interview: What do businesses need to know right now about personal finance?

Jason Howell is a Certified Financial Planner professional and former US congressional candidate in 2019. He was listed as one of the top Wealth Advisors by Washingtonian Magazine. He's also president of the Jason Howell Company, a family wealth management firm that develops regular net worth parents into patriarchs and matriarchs. He does this by walking them through decisions and a unique family governance process. And he's the perfect person to share what businesses need to know right now about finance.

What do people need to know about finance right now?

Initially, I would say know your numbers—which is what you expect a financial advisor to say. But during these times, I'd also say know your legislation.

There was a lot of legislation passed in March 2020. You've heard about the Cares Act, but it's important to note that it was phase three of legislation that had been written very quickly.

A lot has happened with Congress on fiscal stimulus, and a lot has happened with the Federal Reserve on monetary stimulus. In fact, so much so that that's why our markets are doing so well, in large part not because our economy is doing awesome—we all know it isn't. But with so much monetary stimulus, so much happening with the Federal Reserve, there is a lot of money flowing around, and that's called liquidity in credit. What this means is that large companies can do a lot of things. The large companies are the ones that actually move the markets, and they can do a lot of things for many months, that more often than not, they can't do if things tighten up.

While most financial planners will bring to you a specific point of view on how to handle your finances, it's not often you have one that suggests that you have legislative awareness. But it's so critical. New legislation and legislation changes happen—at a rapid pace—and it's important to be knowledgeable and seek expert advice when needed.

What do business owners need to know about finance right now?

Business owners are dreamers. They are people that believe in something, and it's the big reason why they decided not to just take a check as an employee. And what they should know is everything they believed in their dreams is actually possible.

Now that's not just because I'm being a Pollyanna or because we're in America (although being in the right country is really important). But it's because of real numbers.

Work your business in a way that's intentional. Tell yourself that you want to pass wealth down to the next generation of your family. Tell yourself that you want to change the trajectory of your family's last name. And know that it's very possible for you to do that.

The reason that a lot of business owners don't achieve these things is because they haven't been as intentional in growing their business.

For example, I'm in a professional services business, like a lot of people are, and I have to be very intentional about what I'm building. My business is called Jason Howell Company. So, you figure that my business is all about me. But that's not my goal. My goal is 100 years from now, when I'm gone, and my current clients are gone, that this firm will be serving their grandchildren.

And with these big goals in mind, it means you have to do a few things along the way. You might not pay yourself as much. You might have employees when you don't necessarily need to have them (because you could work 12 hours a day), but you want to grow the business in a way that it can be sellable or have something that you can pass down. Keeping that perspective is part of my big idea.

Regular net worth people can become high net worth people in one generation—they just need to know how to do it.

Moving from a regular net worth to a higher net worth is possible, and it begins with knowing your numbers. If you have a really strong knowledge of your numbers, then it becomes much more tangible.

Let me tell you the first thing I do each morning. I turn on my timer to make sure I manage my time, and then I open up all my bank accounts. I may have just done it yesterday, but I look at them all again. I look at those balances. And that makes it serious. That helps you to start building on that practicality from the very beginning. You start to be so aware of your numbers and everything you're doing to impact them. Whether it's time or money, you're very conscious of these things.

My hypothesis has always been that if you're a financial advisor client, you have to be a little ambitious, and you're probably pretty smart, and you are smart enough to know to outsource stuff you don't know. So, I don't have to worry about my clients not being smart enough once I present the opportunity for them, but it has to be presented to them. And once it's presented and the client takes the advice, they realize they are that much closer to the dreams and expectations they have for themselves and their family.

You wouldn't have started your own business if you weren't a bit of a dreamer with some big goals. But making your business intentional takes it a step further and helps you to achieve the big goals you have—such as moving from regular net worth to high net worth.

Do you work with businesses to help bring these concepts and ideas to their employees as well?

I've been fortunate because a lot of times, employers will invite me to come and present to their employees.

I wrote a book that was published last year called *The Joy of Financial Planning*, and so they tell me to bring the book with me, and maybe they pick up a few copies for the staff. And they then have an opportunity to take a deep dive into a lot of the concepts that I understand and that I believe, and so I'll then share that with them verbally. Honestly, a W-2 person is different from a business owner. So, they internalize things a bit differently than the person who's gone out and taken their wits about them and started a company—and I recognize that. That's why I have resources like my book and my podcast, *Joy of Financial Planning*, so that if people are ambitious, they can get the information.

Remember: Know your numbers, and everything is possible for you just as you expected; it's just a lot harder than it was for your parents and your grandparents. You can't just work hard and hope that it will work out. You do need to do things to the best of your financial abilities. My hypothesis is that if you get your finances right and you know what you're doing with your time, you will get everything that you need and most likely everything that you want.

If you have employees that might benefit from the knowledge of a financial planner, consider sharing your resources with them. You could help provide them with the spark to make their dreams a reality.

Three Action Steps

1. Make sure you know your current financial numbers and what changes are happening in legislation to help you make the best decisions.

2. Build your business with intentions that will allow you to achieve your goals.

3. Know that moving from regular net worth to high net worth is possible when you take the right steps and seek experts to assist you.

Connect with Jason at www.linkedin.com/in/jasonhowell/ or calendly.com/jasonhowellcompany/introductory-call

Allow Your Agent to Be a Trusted Advisor

Kieffer Rittenhouse
Vice President, Commercial Insurance Broker
Integrated Insurance Solutions

Kieffer Rittenhouse is a commercial insurance broker for businesses that value service over price. He has been successful in simplifying the buying process and using quality insurance carriers to place coverage.

Main Takeaway

Develop a relationship with your insurance agent so that they fully understand your business and become a trusted advisor to you.

Questions

1. How can businesses save money in today's insurance marketplace?

2. What services are you providing your clients?

3. What can you do for businesses, and do you specialize in certain industries?

Interview: What do businesses need to know right now about insurance?

Kieffer Rittenhouse is a commercial insurance broker for businesses that value service over price. He's been successful in simplifying the buying process and using quality insurance carriers to place coverage. Kieffer is sharing what businesses need to know right now about insurance.

How can businesses save money in today's insurance marketplace?

These last several months, we've worked with a lot of our carriers and a lot of our customers to reduce the costs and reduce their exposures. And as you know, because not everybody had the same sales and payroll and they're pretty big drivers of insurance costs—we reduce those costs, and reduce those exposures with the insurance companies, and help them reduce their overall exposure and financial outlay for cash. Everybody wants cash. That's very critical at this time of year.

If you have fewer employees now because of shifts in your business, then it's going to change your insurance coverage. Make sure you are looking at these things when changes occur.

Several of our carriers gave rebates and money back mid-policy. They knew the utilization of their vehicles and other things were down. So, they were able to give credits before the end of the policy period.

The marketplace is pretty soft. You definitely should rely on your agent to get out there and shop your insurance costs, especially if you're a business with between five and twenty-five employees. There are a lot of carriers that are looking for business, they're dying for business, and they're going the extra mile to reduce your costs and give you a better product.

Everybody's insurance comes up once a year, from a personal line standpoint to a commercial line standpoint. So, you should always test the water and see what's out there. There are a lot of new carriers popping up in our marketplace. It's good to get a number and keep everybody honest.

Take the time every year to look around at what's available and look at what your policy covers.

What services are you providing your clients?

After yesterday's hurricane, right now, I'm in claims mode. I have a couple of people with some claims due to the hurricane that went off the East Coast rather quickly. I'm in the process of helping a client that had a roof on their condo unit that blew off. And I'm in the process of helping out from a coverage standpoint. You definitely want to look at a personal umbrella or business umbrella to give you that extra layer of liability protection. It's a very litigious society that we're in. Having somebody defend you and help you out is pretty critical. So, that's what you're getting when you buy extra coverage in those areas.

One of the toughest parts of my job was telling my clients that there was no coverage for COVID-19. Because it is a pandemic, because it is related to a virus and an illness, there wasn't a lot of coverage. This broke my heart for business owners that didn't have business income that would cover these losses, the downtime, and the closures of their facilities. That was one of the toughest things during this pandemic that has been affecting me has been telling my clients no. A lot of my job is telling clients and providers, "Hey, we could do this, or we can do that . . ." and making them whole on the bottom line when something bad does happen. But, unfortunately, there isn't a lot of coverage out there for this yet. But I think it's going to be something you can buy in the future—and that's exciting.

Change is happening in all businesses—including insurance. While there is currently no coverage that helps businesses cover costs and expenses due to a pandemic, the insurance industry will adapt and change to meet the needs of customers in the future.

What can you do for businesses, and do you specialize in certain industries?

I've spent a lot of time really focused on relationships.

In the old days, I did a lot of cold calling, but now, being in the business for over 25 years, you develop relationships. You develop centers of influence that help guide you to the right people.

I like to try to simplify insurance for my customers and be that person. So, my relationships are what lead me into a lot of these accounts, and then I become an expert by listening to them talk about their business. I do the research about their business and the correct insurance needed.

And then, I look at what they have, and sometimes it's not right for them. I invest a lot of time with my business owners, learning as much about their businesses as possible to make sure that the insurance that they have, and that they've been buying for years, actually fits their business. And a lot of times, it doesn't, and I fix those problems.

I'm working with a client right now in Frederick, and they've been with their agent for a long time. I came in and noticed that they didn't have pollution coverage. And, with their business and what they're doing, and the exposures that they have, pollution is a big concern to their neighbors. If somebody gets sick, and the neighborhood or the water gets contaminated, that's a huge exposure. It would probably put them out of business. But for $15,000 a year, a little over $1,000 a month, they can solve that problem and have somebody defend them and fight the claims and represent them in a court of law. So, it's well worth that premium.

We're trusted advisors. You're not just playing a commodity. You're buying claims rep. You're a risk manager. You're buying a company that will stand with you or next to you when you're facing a claim. You have somebody who's going to defend you, and that's what I am. I'm a trusted advisor.

Your insurance agent is a trusted part of your team. Like others in your expert network, rely on them to bring you their knowledge and skills.

Three Action Steps

1. Have your insurance policy assessed at least once per year to make sure it fits all of the needs of your business.

2. Inform your insurance agent of changes occurring in your business so adjustments can be made to your policy.

3. Make your insurance agent a trusted advisor and part of your expert network.

Connect with Kieffer Rittenhouse at
www.linkedin.com/in/kieffersells/

Health Care Cost Containment

Allison De Paoli
Expert in Healthcare Cost Containment &
Founder of Altiqe Consulting
Altiqe Consulting

Allison De Paoli helps employers take control of their health care spending and get budgeting predictability and the happy side effect of that is better access to high-quality care and lower out-of-pocket costs for their employees.

Main Takeaway

Analyze your healthcare cost data and use that information to help you control the frequency or severity of claims. This may mean looking at alternatives to traditional healthcare plans.

Questions

1. What should businesses be paying attention to when it comes to healthcare costs and claims?

2. If a business has questions about their data, where do they go for more information?

3. What are people doing to control the frequency or severity of their claims?

Interview: What do businesses need to know right now about health plan cost containment?

Allison De Paoli helps employers take control of their health care spending and get budgeting predictability. The happy side effect of that is better access to high-quality care and lower out-of-pocket costs for your employees. And there may be no better time to see what she has to share about what businesses need to know right now about health plan cost containment.

What should businesses be paying attention to when it comes to healthcare costs and claims?

The overriding question is always: What am I doing to control the frequency and severity of my claims? Larger players have had the capability to have that in hand for some time. But now, employers can look at that as well. And it all starts with data.

You know that if you're a small employer (five or eight or twenty employees) and you're fully insured, and you're subject to community rating, your renewal is what your renewal is, right? That's just the way it is. It's designed to protect you, and sometimes it does, and other times it does not.

It's why health insurance costs are such an insane amount of money—because of its community rating. Now you need to understand what you have going on and realize that this may be the time to look at some newer types of services.

Things like direct primary care (DPC), a health share arrangement, or a level self-funded plan may be possibilities. We do them down to five lives.

So even as a small employer, if you look at your data, you can understand what your risk is, and you can manage it.

If you are an employer who provides health insurance coverage for your employees, you know how huge the costs are. The Kaiser Family Foundation released its research from 2019 and found that the average cost of employer-sponsored health insurance for annual premiums was $7,188 for single coverage and $20,576 for family coverage. The report also found that the average annual deductible amount for single coverage was $1,655 for covered workers. These are staggering numbers, especially for small businesses.

If a business has questions about their data, where do they go for more information?

You need to get your data, so ask your advisor for it.

If you run into any questions or if you run into a challenge, you can contact me. We can talk about things that you can do so that you can make good decisions moving forward.

But data is always the first step. More and more data is being collected, and people have access to it, but it's just a piece of the puzzle. You also have to look at what people are doing to control the frequency and severity of their claims.

Have you asked for your data? Have you analyzed it? Do you need assistance understanding it and making good decisions moving forward? Health insurance is a complex industry, and you may need to seek the help of an expert to understand the data. Just as you would seek experts to help in other aspects of your business, don't hesitate to reach out to someone who can help with health care.

What are people doing to control the frequency or severity of their claims?

There are a few things that can be done, and most of them are nontraditional.

One of the things that can be done is changing to direct primary care. Direct primary care is a physician or a group of physicians who have decided to exit the insurance arena. What they do is they set up something that looks like a concierge practice.

It's a fabulous model. What happens is the physician knows that in order to make a reasonable living, and we are talking about a reasonable living, the physician figures how many patients he will take on (generally 400 to 600, maybe 800 patients), and he charges those patients a monthly fee. Usually between $50–$125/month.

This physician manages all of your care. So, if you get the flu, if you need an annual checkup, if you sprain something, or you break something, that is going to be your first stop. Additionally, you generally have 24-hour telephone and text messaging access. And, they do have direct primary care physicians that cover for them if they go away. They charge a small copay when you go into the office for a visit, $10–$20, depending on where you are. That model can handle 80 percent of your medical needs. If you have a cancer diagnosis, you do need health insurance on the back end of that.

Some DPC practices have a pharmacy in-house. They will pass through your prescriptions, usually at cost plus 10 percent. Some of them have x-rays in-house, again at cost plus 10 percent. Some of them have an arrangement with an urgent care clinic or another facility to get your x rays done.

Most of your medical needs can be taken care of right there, especially for things like high blood pressure, diabetes, high cholesterol—as those are easy things to control when they're addressed by a physician.

This DPC model is quickly growing in popularity.

Additionally, telemedicine has exploded. There are several companies that do all of the telemedicine in the United States. Currently, they are mostly maxed out and are having to change their pricing models because of how maxed out they are. I think that's a good problem to have because it is effective care. It is cost-effective care, and it is a cure when it's needed.

Direct Primary Care is gaining in popularity, and it may make sense not only for your finances but for your health to see if DPC is available in your area.

Three Action Steps

1. Ask for your healthcare advisor for your data.

2. Analyze your data to make informed decisions moving forward about health care.

3. Explore alternatives to traditional health care that may help you control the frequency or severity of claims.

Connect with Allison De Paoli at
www.linkedin.com/in/allison-de-paoli/ or www.altiqe.com

Do Your Research on Tax Strategies

Murray Beaulieu
Debt Buster
Boosted Profits

Murray Beaulieu considers himself a "Debt Buster." With 35 years of experience as a manufacturing controller/cost accounting manager for multiple Fortune 500 companies, he now shows businesses how to improve cash flow right with lesser-known but IRS-approved tax strategies and expense saving tactics.

Main Takeaway

Be sure to do your research or seek out an expert to look into all of the tax credits that are available to you and your business. You may be missing out on tax savings—and not even know it.

Questions

1. How can businesses improve their cash flow right now with lesser-known but IRS-approved tax strategies and expense savings tactics?

2. Can you tell us about a tax credit that a lot of businesses might be missing out on?

3. What's one final suggestion you can make to businesses to help them during these times?

Interview: What do businesses need to know right now about tax savings?

What do businesses need to know right now about tax savings is an important topic, and while you may be tempted to only think about taxes when it's time to file your return, it's something you should be thinking about year-round.

Murray Beaulieu has 35 years of experience as a manufacturing controller, cost accounting manager for multiple fortune 500 companies, and in tax and cost remediation. He works to show business owners how to improve their cash flow right now with lesser-known, but IRS-approved, tax strategies and expense savings tactics.

How can businesses improve their cash flow right now with lesser-known but IRS-approved tax strategies and expense savings tactics?

The current conditions have been challenging for all businesses. And, while the government has grandiose plans for stimulus packages, we can all agree that the execution has been less than stellar—to say the least.

And, once again, we can probably all agree that we've never seen anybody get out of debt by having to borrow money. If you got a loan or didn't get a loan—that's okay. There are some things you can look at to help your business.

My favorite no-brainer tax strategy is for anybody who owns commercial property. It's called cost segregation. It's an IRS strategy, and the IRS has actually strengthened this tax code so that you can write off faster.

Cost segregation is a strategic tax planning tool that allows companies and individuals who have constructed, purchased, expanded, or remodeled any kind of real estate to increase cash flow by accelerating depreciation deductions and deferring federal and state income taxes.

Keep in mind that it doesn't matter how old the property is or if somebody who previously owned the property did this before you owned it. (The "clock" on cost segregation starts over when you take ownership of the property.) You can take advantage of this tax strategy.

Also, you will need to have an outside expert look into this for you (do a cost segregation study) as it is backed by engineering principles and usually involves an on-site inspection, as well as a review of building plans, lease agreements, and other records.

Sometimes you need to seek out the help of experts to reap the benefits that are available to you—especially when it comes to tax strategies. Your accountant is one resource, but there are others out there who can assist you too.

Can you tell us about a tax credit that a lot of businesses might be missing out on?

The largest tax credit that is available to any business in the US today is one that over 90 percent of those who qualify for it—don't even apply for—and they should. These are R&D tax credits. This is the largest tax credit available. And this is another one that the government wants you to use as they've increased the benefits of it over the last two tax code changes.

With the R&D tax credits, you need to look at the scope of what all of your employees are doing and see if it meets the IRS definition of "innovation." Now, the definition of "innovation" is a lot broader than you may think. You don't have to have a bunch of guys running around with microscopes and lab coats to take advantage of this tax credit. For example, architecture firms, manufacturing, and software companies—and *many* others—may be able to apply the R&D tax credit to their bottom line if they're willing to ask some questions and investigate the definition of "innovation" according to the IRS.

The incentivization here is you don't make revenue right out of the gate when you're designing something new. It takes time. But the government wants you to keep innovating. So, they reward you by giving you a tax credit in place of the revenue that you're going to get down the road.

Business owners often miss things because they're busy running the day-to-day operations, and they may think certain tax strategies don't apply to them. It never hurts to ask questions! You may be "innovating" and not even know it!

What's one final suggestion you can make to businesses to help them during these times?

One last thing to look at is expenses. At this time, you want to review everything you're paying for.

Your vendors and suppliers don't want to see you go out of business—because when you go out of business, their business feels the effects. They also realize that we're all in the same boat at the moment and that times are tough. Revenue is not being generated like it was in the past. And so, would it pay you to look at your expenses—*all* of your expenses—and negotiate what you're paying? Yes!

For example, do you need a janitor to come in every night? Or could it be cut to twice per week? Do you need your trash picked up weekly when you may not have an office that's fully staffed? Probably not. Do you need the expensive cell phone package for your team that allows for overseas calling when your team is not traveling to Europe at the moment? Can you negotiate your energy contracts? All of these savings can add up and help your business.

It's time to look at things differently.

Sure, you might negotiate when you're buying a car, but what about when it comes to your business expenses? Different times call for different strategies to keep you in business—and negotiating expenses is an out-of-the-box strategy that might save you money.

Three Action Steps

1. Investigate cost segregation as a tax strategy if you own commercial property.

2. Inquire about R&D tax credits and ask if your business might apply these because you are currently working to bring something new to the market.

3. Create a list of all your expenses and negotiate with your vendors and suppliers to reduce them.

Connect with Murray Beaulieu at
www.linkedin.com/in/murraybeaulieu/ and
calendly.com/drmurray/15min for a 15-minute discovery call.

COMMUNICATION

Defy the Status Quo | 119
with Ruthie Bowles

Build Relationships through Emotion | 123
with Susan Rose

Clear, Consistent Communication | 128
with Jennifer McGinley

Be More Than a Walking Business Card | 132
with Rebecca Klein Scott and Keith Scott

Storytelling through Podcasts | 137
with Joey Held

The Experience Economy | 141
with Nathan Willard

COMMUNICATION

Empathy has no script. There is no right way or wrong way to do it. It's simply listening, holding space, withholding judgment, emotionally connecting, and communicating that incredibly healing message of "you are not alone."
—Brené Brown

Empathy is the new normal in business communication. How are you using empathy to authentically connect, communicate, and build relationships? These interviews focus on the communication you use to connect with potential customers as well as share information within your company. During this time, greater communication and empathy are needed to overcome the solitude of quarantine and fear.

Ruthie Bowles of Defy the Status Quo says that your content should qualify or disqualify people. Staying middle-of-the-road will prevent you from standing out. Ruthie talks about communications that lean into empathy but also galvanize your audience.

Susan Rose of Rosebud Communications talks about the place for emotion in communication and marketing. Know your audience, establish your credibility, and use emotion to build connection, relationship, and trust.

Jennifer McGinley of JLM Communications has helped health care organizations navigate crises before, and her message is to be clear and consistent in your communication. Stay ahead of the curve by taking time to gather what you are learning from each experience and don't neglect your internal communications.

Rebecca Klein Scott & Keith Scott of TALLsmall Productions, LLC focus on the words we speak and how we express these through our body language. They have advice for transitioning from in person communication to virtual that works.

Joey Held of Good People, Cool Things takes us into the ever-growing world of podcasting. What works in podcasting and communication in general is storytelling. Stories help us to relate to the material and develop a deeper connection.

Nathan Willard of Ethos Business Guide helps businesses develop experiences for their customers. He shares how we can show that we truly care by taking action and helping our customers to do the same through the experiences we co-create.

Defy the Status Quo

Ruthie Bowles
Podcaster, TV Show Host & Content Creator
Defy the Status Quo

Ruthie Bowles is the founder of Defy the Status Quo, a marketing consultancy. She is a personal brand strategist who focuses on helping social entrepreneurs connect to new audiences using their stories.

Main Takeaway

Determine how you want your business to be perceived, and then create content that helps your business attract the customers and clients you want.

Questions

1. What led you to create your business Defy the Status Quo—and why defiant?

2. How can businesses use content to help them with marketing?

3. Is there a marketing trend this group should keep their eyes on?

Interview: What do businesses need to know right now about being defiant or defying the status quo?

Ruthie Bowles is a podcast host (the Defiant Business Podcast), as well as a television show host, who creates out-of-the-box content strategies for consulting and service firms. Her business is known as "Defy the Status Quo," and she's going to share what businesses need to know right now about being defiant or defying the status quo.

What led you to create your business Defy the Status Quo—and why defiant?

It's never been my style to just get in line.

I had been working as a freelance writer. One day I said to myself, "You know what—there's more to this. There's more to me, and there's a brand here." I brainstormed a lot of different names, but one of the things that really hit me was that I specialize in working with B2B companies. These are usually professional service-type companies. They could be in marketing, consulting, sales, supply chain—those types of companies. And the status quo was that the content was kind of boring for these types of businesses. Yet, what my clients always appreciated about me was that I created content and their strategies that were out-of-the-box. I came up with things that their competitors weren't doing—and that was the key to getting noticed.

Professional sometimes seems to be synonymous with boring. But there's a lot you can do while still maintaining your professional bearing—and not put everyone to sleep. And so that was where it came from.

We are purposely defying the status quo and doing something different.

Has your business become mired in the status quo? Is it keeping you from differentiating yourself and preventing you from thriving? Now may be the ideal time to take a hard look at your business and make sure you're doing all you can to set yourself apart from the pack, so that you get the recognition and notice you need and deserve.

How can businesses use content to help them with marketing?

You need to determine how you want to be perceived.

In my case, I chose "Defy the Status Quo,"—but I had never done a video, for example. I had never created a video and shown my face on LinkedIn, and I was worried. I didn't want it to be somebody just running their mouth for five minutes and then getting off and nobody ever watching it again. And this little thing made me realize, "Okay, I'm defiant." I realized that there were going to be people who don't like this. And that's the point.

In marketing and sales, people talk about, "Oh, let's qualify leads . . ." At the same time that you're qualifying leads, you're also disqualifying others. You're saying this lead is good and this lead is bad.

Your content should do the same thing.

Your content should qualify and disqualify people. For example, if there are people who say, "Oh, I didn't like this new video style she's using. I just don't like it." Then they're not the people for me. Because should I happen to take them on as a client, but then they don't like some of the things I do, I'm going to hear, "Well, we've never done it that way before." And that's a red flag for me—because that's the point. That's why we're doing it right now. You have to be okay with some people not liking you—but that's not really how we like to roll as humans. We want people to like us.

In marketing and sales—and everything you do—you can't talk to everyone. Everybody is not your community, and that is what your content should serve to help you with. It can qualify and disqualify the people who will contact you. And that's a good thing because that means we're not wasting each other's time.

Are you using your content to speak to everyone? Or have you been able to hone your message so that it speaks to the clients and customers you want to attract? You could be spending too much time on people who aren't genuinely interested in your offerings—and it may be time to change your messaging.

Is there a marketing trend this group should keep their eyes on?

Empathy is going to be huge, and this requires a break outside of the norm. For example, on LinkedIn, you're seeing representatives of enterprise-sized businesses showing up in a more genuine manner.

Right now, we're all Zooming, and that means dogs are barking, packages are being delivered, and children are interrupting—and we have to learn how to be empathetic about these things.

How does this apply to your marketing? You don't necessarily have to over-edit or over-polish the content that you're producing. You want it to fit your brand perception.

This is a great opportunity for us as individual professionals and as company representatives to show humanity in our brand. This is a great opportunity to get some individual faces out there.

Empathy has often been discouraged in business, but now is the perfect time to embrace it. Is your business showing empathy? Are you showing your humanity and establishing that connection with your clients and customers?

Three Action Steps

1. Take a look at your business and make sure you are setting yourself apart from your competition by allowing people to see the real you.

2. Create content that attracts the people you want to work with—and does not speak to everyone—so you are not wasting your time and efforts.

3. Use empathy in your marketing to fit your brand's perception and connect with clients and customers.

Connect with Ruthie Bowles at www.linkedin.com/in/ruthie-bowles/ and landing.mailerlite.com/webforms/landing/r5j8j8 to sign up for her newsletter.

Build Relationships through Emotion

Susan Rose
Visibility Coach & Writer
Rosebud Communications

Rosebud Communications provides the full suite of marketing and communications support to nonprofits, associations, and business. Susan has earned praise (and awards) for marketing copy, both print and digital. More importantly, her clients have seen results from her and her team's efforts.

Main Takeaway

Now is the time to position yourself as an expert in your business for your target audience. This is more than just posting to your social media on a daily basis. It's about digging deeper to connect with your audience, not only by educating them but by truly connecting with them.

Questions

1. What do businesses need to be doing to stay visible to their clients and prospects at this point?

2 How do you make yourself/your business stand out

online when there is so much out there for people to choose from?

3. What role does emotion play when it comes to marketing?

Interview: What do businesses need to know right now about thought leadership and content marketing?

More and more people are online than ever before, and more and more time is being spent checking out websites, social media, and various forms of online content. Because this is happening, it's important to look at what businesses need to know right now about thought leadership and content marketing.

Susan Rose is a visibility coach. She helps women entrepreneurs over the age of 50 increase their impact and income in 90 days or less by helping them connect with their audience in a way that increases engagement and builds loyalty. She helps women increase their visibility and become recognized experts, so they can have a greater impact and income by strategically positioning themselves as leaders.

What do businesses need to be doing to stay visible to their clients and prospects at this point?

You want to be creating content and using your social media to drive people to you and your business.

People have more and more time to research you and your business. And they're doing their research and spending this time deciding if your business is actually the kind of business that they want to buy from or work with.

It's not just enough to post to your social media. And, while engagement is good—it's also not enough.

It's about demonstrating your expertise through thought leadership types of materials. These materials might be white papers, longer articles, e-books, or things like these. These materials show your leadership—no matter what business you're in—and will drive people to you and your business.

You might provide some education or training for people who are interested in your business. For example, do a webinar or online workshop to answer questions or address problems that people are grappling with. This shows people that you understand what they're going through and can share answers and solutions with them.

It's really about all the content that is beyond the social media posts.

Now may be the time to take a deep look at what you're sharing on your social media and ask yourself, "Does it really show that I'm an expert in my business? Am I really offering people the materials they need to make an informed decision to work with me?"

How do you make yourself/your business stand out online when there is so much out there for people to choose from?

It's probably been said by every marketing person on the planet, but know who your target audience is. Understand who this person is. Understand who they want to buy from. Understand everything you possibly can about them. And then "talk" to that one singular person directly and in everything that you do.

When you do this, it will resonate with the people you want to do business with. You will be making an emotional bond and an emotional connection with them. You will understand the challenges they are facing. You will understand their journey and how they're going to evaluate if they want to work with you or do business with you.

You don't want to spend your time trying to talk to everybody.

We all know that social media and the internet are flooded with free and/or cheap resources. But do they provide any value? Probably not. If you can understand what your target audience is truly searching for, you can attract them to your business and offer them the solutions they need.

What role does emotion play when it comes to marketing?

At one point in time, when it came to business and emotions—you did not mix the two.

But that mindset has shifted. Emotional does not equal unprofessional. After all, we're human beings seeking a human connection. We respond to emotion. We respond to beauty. We respond to feelings.

If you want people to respond to you, you have to connect with them on an emotional level.

Of course, this is not where you share all the negative things that you may be experiencing or get overly personal. But it is about being honest and authentic. For example, it can be about sharing your excitement about a new service you're launching, why you feel connected to this service, and why you think it will be important to your target audience.

Women are often taught to tamp down that emotional side of themselves, but it can be beneficial in business for creating a connection.

If you're wondering if it's right to share some emotion with your target audience in hopes of creating a connection, start by telling your story. Start journaling, writing it down, or recording it. You don't have to share it if you don't want to—but start talking about it. This allows you to filter through it and decide what is appropriate and what might be too much.

It's about building that relationship with your target audience before you even talk with them or work with them.

How are you creating a connection with your audience? Are you using emotions and authenticity to do it? Or have you avoided this out of fear that it's not the right thing to do in business?

Three Action Steps

1. Create content beyond social media posts that drives people to your business. The content needs to show them that you are the expert that can solve their issue.

2. Figure out exactly who your target audience is so that you can "speak" directly to them online.

3. Share emotion in your marketing that is authentic and creates a connection with clients and potential clients.

Connect with Susan Rose at
www.linkedin.com/in/susanrose001/
susanrose.net/warm-welcome to receive her
"Warm Welcome Email Templates."

Clear, Consistent Communication

Jennifer McGinley
Founder
JLM Strategic Communications

Jennifer helps CEOs and Founders in the health care and education industries amplify their brand and increase impact.

Main Takeaway

Having plans in place for clear and consistent communication builds a strong and solid community.

Questions

1. What do businesses need to know right now about communicating in a crisis?

2. What are people who are communicating successfully doing right now that makes them stand out?

3. What is the benefit of having somebody dedicated to PR for an organization?

Interview: What do businesses need to know right now about public relations in a crisis?

Jennifer McGinley is the CEO of JLM Strategic Communications. She assists CEOs, presidents, and founders in health care, medicine, and education by creating strategic public relations and media campaigns to increase connections, visibility, and credibility. Of course, with all that is happening in the world, she's sharing what businesses need to know right now about public relations in a crisis.

What do businesses need to know right now about communicating in a crisis?

We are definitely reeling from all that is happening currently. People are experiencing pandemic fatigue, as well as Zoom fatigue. And communication can sometimes be tiring. But it's absolutely crucial to stay ahead of the curve.

We're now moving through the crisis. I always say have a plan "A" and a plan "B" and prepare. It's like preparing an editorial calendar. You need to be asking yourself:

- What do you need to think about three to six months out?
- What are things going to look like?

And then plan for that.

Planning is so important for all organizations.

If you were unable to plan for the crisis we're currently in, I hope you've now learned something so that you can take your efforts and clearly communicate effectively moving forward.

For public relations, that starts with internal communications. Everybody in your organization needs to know what's going on at all times. Clear, consistent content and communication build a community. Every organization is a community unto itself. An organization needs to be clear on their who, what, where, when, why, how, purpose, and mission.

Silos within organizations cause a breakdown, and when leadership is not effectively communicating, that's where the breakdown comes in—and the fear. You won't be productive in your leadership efforts, and your employees are going to be afraid and insecure. Giving them a plan for how you're going to be moving forward provides reassurance.

Compassion and empathy are also huge attributes of leaders that will rise above this pandemic and be seen in a positive light.

What are your internal business communications like? Are they effective? Do they make your employees feel valued and included? When you have effective internal communications, you will benefit from faster and more efficient response times during a crisis.

What are people who are communicating successfully doing right now that makes them stand out?

The successful leaders I see are transparent, honest, and tell their employees what the plan is. They want to take care of them and keep them safe. This is really important.

The Y of Central Maryland is an excellent example. Their CEO has done a really beautiful job of sending out wonderful emails to the community and he's grateful and thankful. He did a great town hall meeting, and his passion and warmth came right through the Zoom call. He has the characteristics of a solid leader.

Transparent communication is key at any time, but especially during a crisis. Yet, how does someone go about building that transparency? Ask yourself if you and your team:

- Communicate
- Are honest with one another
- Give each other feedback
- Respect one another
- Admit you are wrong when appropriate

Which of these things are you doing well? Where do you need to put in some work? When these things are happening, you have transparent communication in your business.

What is the benefit of having somebody dedicated to PR for an organization?

I love the term "insourcing." If your organization cannot hire an in-house PR staff, it's best to hire an experienced consultant to help your organization rise above the competition. Without any PR, you risk lacking visibility, consistency, and credibility in your messaging.

When organizations disappear from the public eye, you don't assume the best. You assume the worst.

Not every business can afford to hire an in-house PR person, but there are consultants who work with smaller businesses every day. They can help you stay visible, consistent, and credible—and can be there to help you in a crisis. Do you have a PR person?

Three Action Steps

1. Create a plan for internal communications so that everyone in your business knows what's going on at all times.

2. Ensure that all of your communication is transparent and honest.

3. Enlist the aid of a consultant to assist your business with a PR strategy to help you rise above the competition.

Connect with Jennifer at jlmstrategiccommunications.com/

Be More Than a Walking Business Card

Rebecca Klein Scott and Keith Scott
Founders & Owners of TALLsmall Productions, LLC
TALLsmall Productions, LLC

Rebecca Klein Scott and Keith Scott guide their clients in shaking up how their teams communicate, develop new business, and sustain and create relationships. They work with everyone from Fortune 500 companies to family-owned businesses to individuals.

They show you how to use the tools you already have inside to get "unstuck"—whether it's public speaking, stage fright, anxiety, breaking the cycle of dead-end job interviews, landing a first job, or making a career change.

Main Takeaway

The way you communicate with your words and your body language is a reflection of you and how you are showing up in the moment.

Questions

1. What is the number one thing people can do to improve their communication?

2. What advice do you have for pivoting to communicating in a virtual world?

3. Why does body language matter?

Interview: What do businesses need to know right now about communication?

Rebecca Klein Scott and Keith Scott of TALLsmall use improv style to coach people to harness strong vocabulary and drop filler words that clog the message, tweak body language to a more confident and engaging style, and defuse conflicts. Rebecca and Keith are sharing what businesses need to know right now about communication.

What is the number one thing people can do to improve their communication?

The number one thing is to stop approaching people and introducing yourself as though you are a walking, talking business card. People all of a sudden share these robotic versions of themselves with their name, how long they've been doing it, and their title—and you don't get to meet a person.

And getting rid of all the filler. One of the biggest problems people have is all the "ah, oh, um, like, you know," and all the weak phrases—the "actually" and "would say." The reason that this is a problem is that people become weak. And when you become weak, others can take advantage of you. And to have true leadership, you've got to be strong in your language, strong in your body language, strong in your tone. But many people don't realize the weakness they're showing every day.

Have you equated the "umms" and "wells" as weakness? You can probably think back on conversations where you may not have thought as well of a person because their language didn't necessarily align with what they were saying they did or who they are.

If you were a client, we would bang on the table to make those filler words rise up to the surface because a lot of us don't even realize we're saying them.

What advice do you have for pivoting to communicating in a virtual world?

The number one thing is to schedule breaks. A lot of people book the Zoom calls back-to-back to back. And it requires a lot more mental energy to stare at a screen. We're not used to having to look at ourselves all day, either. That can be awkward, but you can take a Post-it note and put it over your own face, so you don't keep looking at yourself. But taking that break between Zoom calls is critical.

Also, make sure you have a break at the end of the day where you leave—wherever you are living, walk out the door and go somewhere else—I don't care where it is. Because you can get trapped into 12, 14, or 16-hour days and lose it after a while. Rebecca and I, at the end of the day, both go our separate ways and take walks. You've got to make that commitment to drop everything because it's highly addictive. Because you can stay in that same place and then you really lose your efficiency over time.

While we're talking about communication, this is a productivity issue, too—and an efficiency issue. How do you mark the end of your day?

When people don't take breaks, people end up putting the worst part of themselves out there. People need to take breaks. This is a big problem. We're getting more calls to teach work-life balance courses than we ever have before.

Frankly, people look crummy. We get on a session with 30–40 people, and they look tired and disgusted and bored. It's sad to watch this. And I truly believe it's video fatigue. They're not the same people that we remember seeing in person.

Try forgetting about the screen. Stop thinking about it. A lot of people get on a Zoom call, and they'll apologize and say, "Oh, I wish we could do this in person. If we were in person, it would be like this." And when we say that, it makes everybody feel as though this is second best.

Keep people involved as you did in grammar school. Call on people for answers. And make sure if you notice someone that's staring off or maybe not paying attention or whatever, call on them, ask them to ask somebody else a question. But you've got to be like an orchestra leader paying attention to all your instruments. Because if one were to go out of tune, that one next to it also starts to go out of tune, and it's a snowball effect.

We also never use PowerPoint. We start our presentation standing up so that people feel as though we're on a stage. And it helps make people feel as though it's the same as going to an in person workshop. And then we change it up, and we might get the tools out. But we're constantly in motion ourselves. We have different people stand up and do things, and it helps keep people energized.

Do not be afraid—like in a regular meeting, people get up and get coffee, get a cookie, or go to the bathroom. On Zoom, we think we're glued to the seat like we can't leave, but you can leave. You've got to treat it as normal as it was before you just happened to be on a video.

Why does body language matter?

We'll give you an assignment. Go ahead and rub your chin for a moment. When you rub your chin, you lower your heart rate. We need to lower heart rates when we feel anxious, hesitant, or not sure of something. And a lot of people ignore this when they're talking to someone. Let's say we asked you for a raise, and you say, "Sure, I can do that." And if we ignore that body language, you might call us the next day and say, "It's not possible."

And the key is watching that body language because it's 70 percent of everything we communicate.

As someone walks in the door the first time, we make that impression that we all know stays with us forever. It's the same on video calls.

Another thing we noticed with body language, and this is key for people holding meetings, is that you must watch what kind of chair people are sitting in. But if you see somebody sitting in a La-Z-Boy, and they're in the meeting with their feet up, then they are not going to pay attention for very long. The best way to learn is to pay attention to the room. See how people are showing up.

Do you pay attention to the body language of yourself and

others—even in Zoom meetings? Are you aware of the impressions being made?

Three Action Steps

1. Introduce yourself in a manner that allows people to get to know you and remove filler words from your vocabulary.

2. Schedule breaks when communicating virtually to improve communication and productivity.

3. Be aware of your body language and the body language of others to improve your communication.

Connect with Rebecca and Keith at www.linkedin.com/in/rebeccalklein/, www.linkedin.com/in/keithscotttallsmall/ TALLsmallProductions.org

Storytelling through Podcasts

Joey Held
Writer, Podcaster & Musician
Good People, Cool Things

Joey Held is a writer, podcaster, and musician who gives people the tools to tell better stories. He shares these tools, as well as tips on podcasting, writing, and entrepreneurship on his website, Good People, Cool Things. He hopes the site serves as inspiration for creatives to do their own cool thing!

Main Takeaway

Storytelling is a marketing strategy that businesses need to use in order to develop a relationship with their clients.

Questions

1. Why is storytelling so important?

2. What should you look for when honing your message or trying to share it through storytelling?

3. How can businesses use podcasts to share their story and help promote their products and services?

Interview: What do businesses need to know right now about storytelling?

Joey Held is a writer, podcaster, and musician. He shares the tools to tell better stories, as well as tips on podcasting, writing, and entrepreneurship on his website, GoodPeopleCoolThings.com.

If you think that storytelling is only for authors or writers, you're wrong. Storytelling can be used to promote your brand and your business, which is why the topic is so important for business owners. And Joey Held is the perfect person to discuss what businesses need to know right now about storytelling.

Why is storytelling so important?

Think about how many products and services are out there now. With so many different options available, your business needs to be relatable, transparent, and inspiring to get people interested in your product or service.

No longer can you just start shouting, "Hey! Look at me! Look at this!" You want to find a connection with your clients and customers. And for the most part, that connection can be built by sharing your story, sharing how you got to where you are now, how you started your own business, and the things that you've seen along the way.

You need to show you are relatable to your clients and customers. For instance, you're listening to a presentation and the speaker tells you a story about sipping a margarita on top of the Empire State Building. He's there with multiple billionaires and tells you what a great time they had laughing and eating caviar—and what happens? You immediately disconnect from them. It's just not relatable.

But let's pretend you have a computer repair shop, and while your life story may not be relatable to your customers, you can share stories from your business. For instance, someone who came into your shop with a malfunctioning computer and they had no idea what they were doing. They were panicking. They were sobbing—and you helped them with the situation. Most people can relate to a story like that—and you and your business create a connection.

How are you currently communicating with your clients and customers? Emails? Blogs? Social Media? Have you made storytelling a part of your marketing plan?

Forbes Magazine says that storytelling needs to be a priority in marketing for three reasons:

1. Storytelling enables marketers to develop a deeper connection with the audience.

2. Storytelling is a powerful method for learning.

3. Storytelling can be an important tactical tool that lets marketers engage consumers in a fragmented media world.

If you're constantly going for the "sell, sell, sell" approach, you may find it's not working for you anymore—and it's time to make a change.

What should you look for when honing your message or trying to share it through storytelling?

Storytelling should aim to either inspire, educate, entertain—or all three.

When you tell a story that has one or more of these as the goal, it will keep you from rambling and help you to advance your brand message.

Remember, you want to be relatable. This is a huge aspect of brand storytelling. Customers have options for almost any type of business or product they are seeking. Nowadays, they're going to look for the one that appeals to them the most. Storytelling can lead them to you. It's not strictly about price these days, but also connection.

Have you ever had a new client or customer tell you about themselves, and then ask you to tell them a bit about you? They probably weren't doing that as a way of making small talk—even if it seemed that way. They were looking to see if you were relatable, if there was a synergy—because being relatable builds the relationship. And business is about relationships.

Storytelling is just another way for you to have a conversation with your customers—and develop that relationship.

How can businesses use podcasts to share their story and help promote their products and services?

Doing a podcast is really not that different from writing an article—you just have a platform where you can go more in-depth and share more.

Podcasts allow you to go into the details. If you have a podcast with guests, you can start a really nice conversation— especially if the host asks good follow-up questions that help to steer the conversation in a way that allows for stories to be shared. Also, hearing a voice helps to develop rapport.

Storytelling doesn't just have to be about the written word. Podcasts are a great way to share your story. If you're thinking about starting a podcast, take a look at this article that Podcast Insights shared: "How to Start a Podcast: A Complete Step-by-Step Tutorial."

Three Action Steps

1. Review your current strategies for communicating with customers and clients and make sure that story-telling is a part of your plan.

2. Create stories that inspire, educate, entertain—or all three—and share them to build connections with your clients.

3. Research whether a podcast would be a good platform for sharing your story.

Connect with Joey Held at bit.ly/gpctsignup
or at www.linkedin.com/in/joeyheld/

The Experience Economy

Nathan Willard
Writer & Filmmaker, Owner of Ethos Business Guide
Ethos Business Guide

Nathan Willard is a transformative experience developer and practitioner. He uses the skills he's developed as a business owner, filmmaker, writer, and social worker to help mission-driven businesses develop, communicate, and deliver products and services to their customers that their customers truly value.

Main Takeaway

No matter what business you are in, it is more than just selling a product or service. Clients and customers are buying an experience, and they want an experience that is transformative.

Questions

1. What is the experience economy?

2. Why is it important right now for a business to be aware of the experience they are creating for their customers?

3. How do they communicate their story through the experience they provide?

Interview: What do businesses need to know right now about the experience economy?

Nathan Willard is a transformative experience developer and practitioner. He uses the skills he's developed as a business owner, filmmaker, writer, and social worker to help mission-driven businesses develop, communicate, and deliver products and services to their customers that their customers truly value. With his vast experience, he's sharing what businesses need to know right now about the experience economy.

What is the experience economy?

I didn't invent the term "experience economy." There's a book called *The Experience Economy*, and the basic idea is that in the past, we had an economy based on commodities. Then we experienced the Industrial Revolution, and we started to focus on products. Now we've switched to services. And the experience economy takes it a step further.

It's not commodities. It's not about the product or the object that you sell. It's not even about the service that you sell. It's about the experience that you're providing.

The pinnacle example of this is Disney. Anybody who's ever been to Disneyland or Disney World or encountered Disney at all understands that Disney is not just about products or services; it's about the entire experience that they provide for their customers.

So, the basic idea is that no matter what your business is, realize that what we're actually selling is the experience. And our customers want transformative experiences. This is something we need to realize now, and no matter what the future brings, that's something that we need to always be paying attention to—no matter what our business is.

Have you put any thought into the experience you are providing for your customers? While initially, you might be able to provide them a product or service they need, eventually, that will not be enough with the number of choices that consumers have available.

Why is it important right now for a business to be aware of the experience they are creating for their customers?

Most people have had it drilled into their head that you're not supposed to be selling features; you're supposed to be selling benefits. And that means explaining what you do and if it's a product, to explain the benefits to the customer.

Now we're moving to selling the experience. And while I don't know that it's more important than ever—it definitely has applications today.

We have two major crises happening at this moment. One is COVID-19, and the other that is happening has to do with the riots, the police, and the political world. So, every business needs to consider how these are going to affect their clients.

When you're working with your current customers or trying to attract new customers, you have to think about the fears, the concerns, and the problems that your customers have. And if you're not thinking about those things, then you're not thinking about how they're affected by COVID-19 or how they're affected by the political unrest that is occurring right now.

Your clients and customers are greatly affected by the things happening outside of your business. Have you thought about this as you interact with clients? Have you tied it to the experience you are creating for them?

How do they communicate their story through the experience they provide?

You have examples of businesses who have destroyed or ruined their business because their owner or CEO makes some stupid joke on Twitter. They think it's funny, but it can ruin their business.

This isn't just about pretending that you care. It is about being aware of how your actions affect people, how they're going to affect your business, and realizing that that is all part of what your business is about.

The current atmosphere and your actions are going to affect how people see your business. It's going to affect the character of your business and how you're perceived. And how you respond in these kinds of situations matters to people. Or, if you fail to respond, that also matters to people, and they will notice it.

Nobody gets to pretend that they don't have to care about these things. You have to take some sort of action.

The experience goes beyond the experience you're creating for your customers, clients, and employees. You also need to consider the experience that they're having in the larger world and how your company fits into that puzzle.

Three Action Steps

1. Establish the experience that you are trying to bring to your customers.

2. Be aware of fears, concerns, and problems that your customers are facing, so you know how they affect your customers.

3. Create a response to the concerns and problems that shows you care about what your clients are facing.

Connect with Nathan Willard at www.linkedin.com/in/
nathan-a-willard/
or nathanwillard@ethosbusinessguide

CONNECTION & COLLABORATION

Establish Partnerships | 149
with Elizabeth Dodson

Virtual Networking | 154
with Jim Ries

Utilize Emotional Brand Intelligence | 158
with Mark Firth

Be Yourself on Camera | 163
with Brighton West

Build an Alchemy Network | 167
with Dov Gordon

CONNECTION & COLLABORATION

Individually, we are one drop. Together, we are an ocean.
—Ryunosuke Satoro

When your primary focus is building relationships, then your focus shifts from competition to collaboration. These next interviews highlight how to connect and collaborate to grow your business, taking into account that networking and business, in general, has moved into the online space. We look at the tools you can use and how to transition in person into virtual without losing the quality of the interaction.

Elizabeth Dodson of HomeZada focuses her energy on partnerships to leverage the time and skill sets of everyone involved. She explains how to find partners and how to ensure that the relationship works well for everyone.

Jim Ries of Offit Kurman is a master networker who prides himself on being able to make meaningful connections. When the pandemic sent everyone home, networking had to shift as well. Jim shares how to create relationships in the virtual world.

Mark Firth of the Linkpreneurs has taken relationship building to social media, first with LinkedIn and now with Facebook. What he found is that developing these relationships takes emotional brand intelligence, which starts from a place of curiosity. He shares how to use the vast amounts of information on LinkedIn to create authentic relationships.

Brighton West of Brighton West Video shares the importance of being yourself on video and how to create connection using video technology. Just turning on the camera is not enough. However, you can start by showing up even when you are nervous.

Dov Gordon of Profitable Relationships explains how to use the relationship building you have been doing for free to create a new revenue stream.

Establish Partnerships

Elizabeth Dodson
Co-Founder of HomeZada
HomeZada

Elizabeth Dodson and HomeZada serve homeowners interested in managing the details of their homes, like tracking their home inventory, managing a maintenance calendar, and projects, so that they have better financial awareness. She also works with companies that service homeowners like those in real estate, insurance, builders, and mortgage, to retain and engage their existing customers while gaining new customers.

Main Takeaway

Creating partnerships can help you to increase your customer base or provide more value to your existing customers.

Questions

1. Why is partnering with other companies potentially important to business?

2. How do you find companies to partner with?

3. What are the keys to building successful partnerships?

Interview: What do businesses need to know right now about partnerships?

Elizabeth Dodson is the co-founder of HomeZada. Elizabeth and her company serve homeowners interested in managing the details of their homes, like tracking their home inventory, managing their maintenance calendar, and projects , so that they have better financial awareness.. They work with companies that service home-owners like those in real estate, insurance, builders, and mortgage, to retain and engage their existing customers. Elizabeth is sharing what businesses need to know right now about partnerships.

Why is partnering with other companies potentially important to business?

Partnering actually benefits a lot of different organizations.

In our case, specifically, we have a lot of partners who want to continue to retain their customers and provide value as it relates to customer service, and yet, HomeZada wants to reach more customers, and specifically homeowners. And we can do that really efficiently with partners.

This also applies to other organizations when they're considering how to grow their business. Partnerships can either accelerate their time to get to consumers or whoever the customer is, or it can actually help them provide more value to their customers, and that's what we look for in these relationships.

Have you looked to find partners for your business? Partners who can be a value-add to your existing business or can help you grow? Steve Jobs said, "Great things in business are never done by one person; they're done by a team of people."

How do you find companies to partner with?

Whomever you're trying to partner with, I would recommend looking in specific trade publications. You can go on LinkedIn because there's the search functionality in LinkedIn—and we all love LinkedIn.

Additionally, reach out to your colleagues and your network, see who else knows somebody.

So, in our case, when it comes to real estate, mortgage, insurance and homebuilding type organizations, we reach out through trade publications. We find them when we speak at events, whether it's virtual or in person, and we build those relationships.

And, at the same time, we also reach out via LinkedIn to find folks as well as use our network.

One of the other things that we also do is reach out to organizations that offer specific consulting services to specific industries. And those organizations are also looking at new concepts to provide their customers. Often, a lot of that has to do with something like HomeZada. And so, we form relationships with organizations and specific divisions in those consulting companies. They can then recommend HomeZada. This also ties into how you extend your brand, and in our case, beyond that transaction, and using HomeZada can actually help them do that.

Have you brainstormed who also knows the customer that you're trying to reach and is working with them? When you know your ideal customer, you can then look to see who is also working with that customer and see how partnerships can be created.

What are the keys to building a successful partnership?

Everyone's got partnerships, and you want to make sure that they are successful as they can be. Some will work out, and some won't. But you never know until you try. And we're firm believers in that.

One of the things we look at—whether we're doing marketing or whether we're doing partnerships—we look at setting the appropriate expectations. That's the first step. So, each party has to come to the table with the appropriate expectations of what they need from the relationship.

Then we measure the expectations and figure out if we achieved those expectations. And some of these relationships will last for a very long time.

You will also need to adapt and adjust those expectations and those measurements. And so, it's important to keep that information constantly evolving and moving, and also to measure it.

And I know a lot of folks build relationships by saying, "I have this great friendship with somebody . . ." and it's fantastic, and that's really important. However, if the relationship is not providing value to all the different parties, then it can actually become too costly. So, you want to make sure that you're not in that position either.

My skill set and background are in business development and partnerships, and making sure that those relationships can stay successful was one of the things I was really proud of, because how do we do that knowing that these partnerships are so varied and vastly different? And it goes back to setting those expectations, having the measurements, having those discussions with your partners, and then at the same time, adjusting and evolving those expectations and measurements for times, like the one we're in right now.

Now more than ever is a great time to build relationships. There are definitely ways to still open those lines of communication and build the relationship. Having partnerships provides an extra buffer when things are tumultuous because now it's not just your business, it's your business partnered with another business, and there is strength in that relationship.

Remember, your relationship with an individual at a company may change. For example, if you work with a large company, individuals move to different roles very quickly. So, it's important to make sure that you're not only managing that relationship with the individual, but you're also building other relationships with other individuals in the company, and you have documentation of those measurements, should you get a new person who you need to talk to.

Three Action Steps

1. Establish partnerships as a way to increase your customer base or provide a value-add for your existing customers.

2. Brainstorm who is working with your ideal customers right now and what kind of partnerships you can establish with these businesses.

3. Create expectations and measurements to ensure that the partnerships are beneficial.

Connect with Elizabeth Dodson at www.linkedin.com/in/edodson
or www.homezada.com/contact

Virtual Networking

Jim Ries
Director of Business Development
Offit Kurman

Jim Ries is Director of Business Development at Offit Kurman. They are a full-service law firm, serving the legal needs of small and mid-size, privately held, owner-managed businesses, with 230 attorneys in 14 offices from Charlotte to New York City, with a heavy concentration in the Maryland/DC/Northern Virginia region. Jim has access to a deep network of attorneys in every practice area, and he connects business owners to the right attorney who can resolve their legal disputes and protect their assets. Jim is a master networker, and he prides himself on being able to make meaningful connections.

Main Takeaway

Embrace virtual networking and figure out a way to incorporate it into what you do.

Questions

1. Why do you need to network virtually?

2. How can you leverage social media to help with your virtual networking

3. What should you do when attending a virtual event?

Interview: What do businesses need to know right now about virtual networking?

Jim Ries is Director of Business Development at Offit Kurman. They are a full-service law firm, serving the legal needs of small and mid-size, privately held, owner-managed businesses, with 230 attorneys in 14 offices from Charlotte to New York City, with a heavy concentration in the Maryland/DC/Northern Virginia region. Jim has access to a deep network of attorneys in every practice area, and he connects business owners to the right attorney who can resolve their legal disputes and protect their assets. Jim is a master networker, and he prides himself on being able to make meaningful connections. Jim is sharing what businesses need to know right now about virtual networking.

Why do you need to network virtually?

People still want to connect, and virtual networking gives us the opportunity to connect and continue to build relationships. Webinars have replaced seminars. Zoom meetings have replaced networking events. And phone calls have replaced coffee meetings. We all miss the in person networking, but there's no sense complaining about it. We must really embrace what we have. And we've got to play the hand that we've been dealt. Remember, this is a marathon, not a sprint. This is going to take some time, but don't complain about where we are with this virtual networking stuff. Embrace it and figure out how to work it in with what you do.

When it comes to virtual networking, I like to combine a business development aspect, networking aspect, and an educational aspect into an event. Those are the events that I prefer. I've actually got a couple of my own that I've launched since the pandemic, and they seem to be pretty popular, but it really needs to include those three elements.

How can you leverage social media to help with your virtual networking?

I say don't social distance from social networking and social media. You need to be active on social media, and if you have a B2B business, LinkedIn is the best platform where you really need to be active.

Don't be what we call a lurker. A lurker is someone who goes on LinkedIn and reads stuff and might click like here or there, but that's not really being engaged. You really need to share your own relevant content. You need to add comments to people when they post stuff that's meaningful to you. Share content that's meaningful to you and to your network. So, don't be a lurker—get involved.

Social media is fine. You know people buy from people that they know, like, and trust. And by using social media, you can get to the know and the like part. But to get the trust, you really need to go deeper. And after you connect on social media via, let's say LinkedIn, for example, then it's time to maybe schedule a phone call or a Zoom meeting, and really start building the trust and try to cultivate the relationship. You can't just do that with these quick interactions on social media. So, use it to accomplish the know and the like, and then and then trust is achieved after cultivating the relationship. And remember, this is a marathon, not a sprint.

There are lots of people who are so eager right now to jump onto social media, especially LinkedIn. They know people are doing business on LinkedIn, and instead of that marathon, they're thinking of it as a sprint. They jump in immediately with, "Can I get on the phone with you? This is what I offer." Don't forget that part that you naturally have in a face-to-face interaction, where you say hello and introduce yourself and get to know the person. Build the relationship.

What should you do when attending a virtual event?

It's very much like in person networking. So, the first thing you do is arrive early and meet the host and the presenter. Get to know them. Get familiarized with them and get there before everybody else.

Understand who the audience is going to be. Think about if this is a membership organization or Chamber of Commerce. Think about who is going to be in that audience and be ready to introduce yourself in a meaningful way to the audience.

Again, don't be a lurker, be an active participant and provide some meaningful commentary. Go in with a story. Ask people you know how they're doing during the pandemic but share a good story.

Connect with the attendees on LinkedIn with a personal message after you've met them. And then maybe invite them for a phone call or video chat.

Focus on them when you go to these events. Focus on them—not on you. Be interested, not interesting. Be curious, ask questions, and then, when they say "tell me about you," then they've given you permission to tell you all about yourself and your business.

Most importantly, remember to follow up. Otherwise, you are wasting your time. So, follow up with the people you meet. Don't go in expecting to meet thirty people. Go in expecting to walk away with three good potential follow-ups. That's my magic number.

Using this process to participate in virtual networking events allows you to institute some best practices. Remember that the technology makes it different, but so much of it is the same as in person events.

Three Action Steps

1. Use virtual networking as an opportunity to connect and build relationships.

2. People do business with people they know, like, and trust. Proper use of social media can accomplish the know and like. Trust is achieved after cultivating the relationship.

3. Arrive early to virtual networking events. Get to know your host and make meaningful commentary with the focus being on getting to learn about people—and be sure to follow-up and stay in touch.

Connect with Jim Ries at
www.linkedin.com/in/jries/ JRiesoffitkurman.com
or call at 410-733-6133.

Utilize Emotional Brand Intelligence

Mark Firth
Founder
The Linkpreneurs

Mark Firth helps business owners book calls, land ideal clients, and change their life in 90 days using emotional brand intelligence.

Main Takeaway

LinkedIn as a platform is about building relationships in a genuine and authentic manner.

Questions

1. What's causing the current influx of people to LinkedIn right now?

2. What changes have you seen in LinkedIn from last year to this year?

3. How do you "break in" or start conversations?

Interview: What do businesses need to know right now about LinkedIn?

Mark Firth helps solopreneurs consistently book qualified calls using LinkedIn combined with emotional brand intelligence. He's been doing it since 2017, and he's the person you need to know if you're trying to generate leads on LinkedIn. Mark is sharing what businesses need to know right now about LinkedIn.

What's causing the current influx of people to LinkedIn right now?

I think it's a combination of two things externally. Obviously, the events, meaning that we can't do as many stage events and we can't go network as much. With the "no contact economy" that I've heard it described as, it means LinkedIn is the natural alternative.

The second thing, which not so many people know, is that on June 1, 2020, LinkedIn got a new CEO, Ryan Lansky. He quickly made a lot of changes to the platform. They're moving the platform. They changed the content algorithms to be the same as Facebook. They tried to change engagement in the feed. So basically, and I'm not a betting man, but if I was, they are modeling the Facebook model, but for business, and we know that works.

That's why I think people are going on there and not only going on there—they're spending more time on there.

LinkedIn is definitely undergoing a series of transitions. Do you like them? Have you found yourself spending more time on the platform? Is it working for you and your business?

Stories are coming, and that is not a secret. They've spoken about it, and basically, this is going to help transition from the messenger part of the application to the content feed. And that's just a natural progression you see on all platforms.

What changes have you seen in LinkedIn from last year to this year?

I think the main change has been this—many people have gone to the platform, and we're in the internet marketing world, which I'm certainly a part of—even though I try not to be. But the reality is, people push tactics. They push all these ideas that work at the time, but then everyone starts doing it, and then the people on the platforms get tired of it.

So, I think the example of that on LinkedIn was in 2017, and that's when automation started. And if you're watching and don't know what automation is, it means you send the same message in a sequence to everybody regardless of who they are—and you sit back on your sofa. As with anything, when something's new, it works. When a tactic is new, it works. But when everyone's doing it then becomes noise, and noise, by default, is ignored.

LinkedIn has also changed very much in the last six to twelve months in terms of people looking for more personal connections on the platform—that kind of not getting sucked into the pitches and the good copywriting. They want to build a relationship. I just read Russell Brunson's new book, *Traffic Secrets,* which is fantastic. By the way, I have no affiliation with it, but he was talking about if you want to be successful on a platform, you want to go with the flow of what the platform wants, and LinkedIn wants to build authentic relationships. It doesn't want you to spam the hell out of your audience. Just go with it in the long term.

Relationship building seems to be the way right now. People are using storytelling to build relationships. Are you using LinkedIn to build relationships?

When it comes to utilizing LinkedIn, I've got a little story or an analogy to share. I want you to imagine it's pre-you know what's going on at the moment, and we're in a busy downtown on a Wednesday afternoon. We go into a bank, and there's a line of people waiting to see the teller. If you walk to the front of that line and stand in front of the first person without saying anything, you're going to upset some people, right? That's just not how people do things. Now, let's replay that scenario. Let's imagine you walk into that same bank. You've got a two-year-old in your arms and you're pushing a stroller with a kid crying, and your dog is outside on the railing barking. You look at everyone in line and say, "I'm terribly sorry, you don't have to do this, but we're in a rush. We're on the way to grandma's, and I don't want to inflict these screaming kids upon you for 20 minutes. Would we be able to just jump to the front of the line?" You're not guaranteed a favorable response, but certainly, the probability is higher, and the difference between those two scenarios is this context for the action.

LinkedIn is very different from Facebook or any social media platform. Because of the amount of information in the profiles and the amount of access you can get to people's posts and content, and who they follow is—it is very distinct. And, in that respect, that gives us a ton of context to start conversations. You've got thousands of words and data points, and you know what they've been doing for the last 10 years. My advice is to use context to start the conversation. Look at their profile, ask them a question about something they did in the past, in which you have a genuine interest. You can't go wrong.

Start by being curious and interested and move forward like you would if you actually met that person in real life.

Our brains haven't changed that much in a few millennia. Relatively speaking, we still have the same needs, wants, and desires and the desire to feel needed and not want to be rejected and not want to feel taken advantage of. So, instead of looking for these cheap tactics and the message that was for everyone, just base your message on real-life—it's as simple as that.

How do you "break in" or start conversations?

So, we've dealt with introverts, extroverts, and everything in between. I test on Myers Briggs. Some days I test INTP; other days, I test ENTP. I'm right in the middle. I get it, and we've had all sorts.

It's ultimately about getting the right help. And it's not looking for that silver bullet. There is no silver bullet for lead generation. People sell a recipe when you need a cookbook. That cookbook needs to involve mindset. It needs to involve awareness of your personality. It needs to involve awareness of your blind spots, getting out of your comfort zone. You need all sorts of stuff to create that cookbook and take all those little bits out of it if you've been going for the silver bullet of LinkedIn lead generation.

Lead generation is a new class. I've been in sales lead generation since 2003. There is no silver bullet—it doesn't exist. What exists is hard work and self-awareness. That's where emotional branding comes in.

Because you're right, if you're an introvert, you're aware of that, and then you've got a huge advantage because you do things in a certain way.

A lot of the market talks about "Yeah, I'll get you 10 to 20 meetings, autopilot lead generating machine . . ." and all that. And they're talking about external things, but everything begins with you. It's as simple as that. If you don't have the emotional intelligence, the emotional brand intelligence to know the way you should behave is congruent with your brand, congruent with what you're selling, and indeed in alignment with your personality and your strengths, you're going to struggle. Because if you're introverted, and someone's asking you to do extrovert stuff, I don't care who you are; it's going to be difficult; it's not in your zone of genius. Have that awareness of who you are, and then combine it with all the external stuff.

Three Action Steps

1. Use the vast amount of information available to you on LinkedIn to create authentic relationships with the people you are connecting with.

2. Avoid messaging that is designed for everyone and, instead, focus on messaging that connects with individuals.

3. Utilize your emotional brand intelligence to remain in alignment with your personality, your brand, and your strengths.

Connect with Mark Firth at www.markfirthonline.com

Be Yourself on Camera

Brighton West
Virtual Videographer
Brighton West Video

Brighton West is a Virtual Videographer helping professional coaches market their practice and spread their message using online video. He makes creating authentic and professional videos easy and fun! Video is perfect for client testimonials, YouTube videos, and video headshots. When you work with him, everything is done virtually through your webcam. No scary equipment or video studios—everything is done from the comfort of your home or office.

Main Takeaway

Get yourself on camera and be authentic—even if it's not perfect.

Questions

1. What kinds of tools or resources do we need in order to be doing video?

2. How important is it to show up on video, and what should you be saying?

3. How can you create that connection when you're doing a video?

Interview: What do businesses need to know right now about using video?

Are there any businesses nowadays that aren't using video in some way, shape, or form to reach out to their clients and customers or stay connected with their employees? Probably not. Video seems to be the go-to medium. And it has so many applications that it's truly not surprising. Brighton West is a videographer. He works with professional coaches to create videos they can use to market what they do and spread their message—and it's all done virtually—using webcams and smartphones. It only makes sense that he's here to share what businesses need to know right now about using video.

What kinds of tools or resources do people need in order to be doing videos?

Right now, everyone is making a shift—and we're making it together. And currently, people crave connection more than anything. Videos are really the only way we have to make this connection.

I always used to recommend the Logitech C920 or C922 webcams. But they're currently unavailable. And really, is the camera the important thing? No . . . you just need to get on camera. You just need to go for it. And you need to say, "Whatever happens, happens."

You might start to piece together equipment as you go along, but don't let a lack of equipment stop you from making video happen.

Going on camera for the first time can be nerve-racking, but some-times you just need to jump in with both feet and make it happen. Embrace the imperfect!

How important is it to show up on video, and what should you be saying?

It's definitely important that you are showing up on video right now.

While Zoom burnout is a real thing, you still need to be using video to create a connection.

Don't worry about being super polished—just say what is authentic to you right now. We need to have relaxed conversations. You need people to feel like you're a friendly voice—which is probably even more important than having amazing content.

People really want to connect with people.

And remember, it's easier to be on camera all day long when it feels more natural. This may mean having a setup at home that allows you to see who you are talking with, along with seeing how you look at the moment.

When you're doing a video, remember that the human connection you are trying to make outweighs being perfectly polished while speaking or presenting amazing content. People want to see you and feel you. If you stumble over your words or have tech issues, don't worry. We've all had those things happen—and they make you very relatable.

How can you create that connection when you're doing a video?

When you're on camera, you need to look into the camera lens for the other person to feel like you're connecting with them. If you're looking down at them on the screen, it looks like you're not connecting. But if you can be that person who shows up and looks them in the eye—that's so much better. The connection will be there.

It can be exhausting to know where to look during a video conversation. Do I look at the person I'm talking with? Do I look at the green light?

If you can create a setup that allows you to look at people in the eye—you'll find that sense of connection improves drastically.

Currently, I use a teleprompter app (which is typically used to scroll text in front of the screen) to project the image that's in front of the camera. I can now easily see who I'm speaking with and myself—and it's not weird or awkward. (This setup does require an external webcam.) If you don't have a setup like this, you may find it easier to do a video on a cell phone.

Remember those in person conversations we used to have regularly? And how you always looked someone in the eyes to show that you were engaged and listening? The same goes for video. Look the person in the eyes as much as possible—it will make them feel valued and connected.

Three Action Steps

1. Start connecting with people using video—even if you're nervous or not sure what to say.

2. Be authentic on camera. You can create a connection by being a friendly voice in a sea of noise.

3. Create connections with people by looking them in the eye—just like you would with an in person conversation.

Connect with Brighton West at:
www.linkedin.com/in/brightonwest/
and brighton@brightonwestvideo.com for a free 30-minute session with him.

Build an Alchemy Network

Dov Gordon
Owner & Creator of Profitable Relationships
Profitable Relationships

Dov Gordon, of ProfitableRelationships.com, helps consultants use "backwards" networking to reach their ideal clients—consistently. Experienced consultants know that the best clients come from referrals and relationships. But referrals are unpredictable. And relationships take lots of time. Instead, Dov helps you become an "under-the-radar" leader in your industry. It gets better because Dov shows you how to leverage the relationship marketing you've been doing for free—into a six-figure revenue stream. It's all at ProfitableRelationships.com.

Main Takeaway

Building an "alchemy network" allows you to get beneath the surface and build relationships that you can leverage to build your business and create an additional revenue stream.

Questions

1. What do business owners need to know now about building their own network?

2. How do you become an "under-the-radar" leader in

your industry?

3. Can you really turn the relationship marketing you're doing from a time sink into a revenue stream? If so, how?

Interview: What do businesses need to know right now about building their own network?

Dov Gordon, of ProfitableRelationships.com, helps consultants use "backwards" networking to reach their ideal clients—consistently. Experienced consultants know that the best clients come from referrals and relationships. But referrals are unpredictable. And relationships take lots of time. Instead, Dov helps you become an "under-the-radar" leader in your industry. It gets better because Dov shows you how to leverage the relationship marketing you've been doing for free—into a six-figure revenue stream, and it's all at ProfitableRelationships.com. Dov is sharing what businesses need to know right now about building their own network.

What do business owners need to know now about building their own network?

I think you need to know that your unfair advantage, and we all need an unfair advantage, is your relationships with the right people. So, the right relationships are your unfair advantage. And exactly what that means will vary from person to person and from business to business. But it's probably not your Facebook ad, although that is definitely valuable, but it is your relationships.

When it comes to building relationships, I've been doing this for myself for the last 10-plus years, and I've been recently (in the last really half a year—plus or minus) helping others to do, is to start what I call an "alchemy network."

That could be you form a network that's either of colleagues or your ideal clients or recommenders. And then, according to everybody's situation, you've got to think through what makes the most sense for you.

But just like owning the casino, the house has an advantage when you own the network. You have many advantages.

And I've been helping people, mostly consultants, start their own alchemy network. This gives them an advantage when reaching out to potential clients for one thing or another or people they are looking to reach, and it enables you to create leverage in everything you're doing. Because most consultants will tell you that their best clients have come through referrals or relationships.

Now referrals you don't have much control over. And relationships take a lot of time. It's just the way it is. So, what I developed is this idea of an alchemy network. It developed over time, and it's something that I didn't set out to figure out and that I brainstormed one day. But it's something that I slowly figured out, and I'd been doing it for myself, and it's been the main source of my clients over the years.

It enables you to create leverage in your relationship building and consistency in referrals. It's not a networking group per se. It's not a Business Networking International, (BNI) type thing.

Obviously, anytime you get to bring people together, there are commonalities. But there are nuanced differences that really make it what I've come to think about as an alchemy network. This is the idea of alchemy—the art of turning lead into gold, in theory—and it's about getting beneath the surface.

Imagine the alchemists of old. They weren't thinking, "Oh, I could just turn lead into gold." They probably thought, "If we can get to the underlying structure of the lead, we can leverage it and turn it into something more valuable into gold."

And it's the same thing. We can't turn lead into gold, even with our powerful microscopes and who knows what today. But what we can do is stop skidding across the surface and get beneath the surface. And that's what this is all about. It's about getting beneath the surface of all those people that you know and bringing the right ones together so that you can leverage it.

Do you have an "alchemy network" that allows you to leverage your relationships and get referrals to assist your business? How did you go about building it? How did you nurture it, so it wasn't a "surface-level" group, but one that was robust and valuable?

How do you become an "under-the-radar" leader in your industry?

I've been doing this for 10-plus years, and I've got two networks that I lead now. And honestly, I used to think, "Well, this is so easy—anybody could do it." And it didn't really occur to me to help anyone else do it.

But in the last couple of years, I started to think about it. And I started to realize, "Oh, actually, I might be stricken with the expert's curse,"—where what's easy to me is not so easy for others. And I've come to see this with the more people that I've been helping. They asked me a question about this or that, and I realized that is a big part of the value. It's the small details. It's the nuances and the mastery—that's what makes the difference between someone who hasn't had the experience of all the various things I've done over the years. They might have one question that can make them just stop or get stuck, and that's really a big part of it. It's quite fascinating and exciting.

All of us, as we go along in our business, have that turning point where we go, "Oh, this thing that comes so easily to me, that I take for granted, is not easy for other people." And it's the thing that you need to leverage.

Can you really turn the relationship marketing you're doing from a time sink into a revenue stream? If so, how?

That's one of the most interesting or exciting parts about this. If you are a consultant or some kind of expert and most of your clients are coming through referrals and relationships of some kind, then you're spending a lot of time cultivating those relationships already. And when you create your own alchemy network, you turn that into a revenue stream. Without a lot of exaggeration, it could become an additional $50,000 a year, or $100,000 or $200,000 a year, from getting paid for doing things that you're largely doing already. And that's the magic of it.

If you're doing this, you not only have an unlimited source of clients, but they're paying you to connect to other people in your network. And it's something that allows you to leverage the time that you're already spending to build relationships.

The most surprising thing about these networks is that everybody has a story. Everybody needs something. And one of the things that holds us back is thinking that "I'm different." We're all different, and we're all the same, and you've got something that people need.

Three Action Steps

1. Create an "alchemy network" that allows you to leverage your relationships in ways that benefit your business.

2. Understand what "comes easy" to you and how you can leverage that to be of value to others.

3. Utilize your "alchemy network" to be an additional revenue stream for you.

Connect with Dov Gordon at www.linkedin.com/in/dovgordon/ or dovgordon.net/nettie to get "The Plenty of Clients Manual."

PEOPLE

Recruiting | 176
with Jennifer Mastor

Hiring | 180
with Jennifer Mastor

Value Your People | 184
with Bob Graham

Business & Mental Health | 189
with Fred Chanteau

PEOPLE

Employees are a company's greatest asset—they're your competitive advantage. You want to attract and retain the best; provide them with encouragement, stimulus, and make them feel that they are an integral part of the company's mission.

—Ann M. Mulcahy

Bringing in the right people and then caring for them as the biggest asset in your company means starting from a process that works to align with those right people. Then, give them an environment where they can thrive and support them as human beings.

Jennifer Mastor of MASTOR Recruiting and Consulting gives us the tools and information we need to continue to recruit even while businesses still operate virtually.

Jennifer Mastor continues with hiring from the candidate's perspective as it is important to understand both sides of the table.

Bob Graham of Breakthrough Solutions digs into the value companies put on people, how to create trust, and how to develop a shared company vision with every person in your organization.

Fred Chanteau of the Affiliated Santé Group draws from his deep knowledge of mental health and crisis services from over 45 years in the industry. He shares how to care for your employees and to be vigilant for the signs of stressors that can impact their well-being and work.

Recruiting

Jennifer Mastor
Owner & Professional Recruiter
MASTOR Recruiting and Consulting

Jennifer represents companies of all sizes that need to hire front and back-end individuals. She recruits for entry-level to "C" Suite for all positions, with the exception of IT and medical roles. Additionally, she helps support individuals who need assistance with career decisions.

Main Takeaway

Asking good questions of your candidates during the hiring process will help to ensure they're a good fit for your business.

Questions

1. Should businesses be recruiting right now?

2. What are the soft skills that companies should be looking for in candidates?

3. What questions should you ask your candidates, and what questions should you be asking your current employees during this time?

Interview: What do businesses need to know right now about recruiting?

With lots of companies laying off at the moment, is it really the right time to talk about recruiting? Jennifer Mastor is a professional recruiter. She represents companies that need to hire unique and intelligent individuals who already have soft skills and know how to use them. Additionally, she represents individuals who want to find their next career. And she's an excellent resource for what do businesses need to know right now about recruiting.

Should businesses be recruiting right now?

Absolutely. Absolutely. This is not stopping companies at all.

There are considerations to take into account. If you are interviewing someone who has been laid off, you need to know why they were laid off. Was it because they should've been laid off before the pandemic happened? Or were they laid off because the pandemic happened, and their company truly did not want to lose them?

Employers should definitely be interviewing a lot differently right now. They need to be asking some solid skills questions and soft skills questions. Soft skills questions are a big factor in the hiring process right now, and businesses need to be asking about them and taking advantage of it.

While you may not think this is the time to be hiring, if your business is continuing to operate as usual, you may find some fantastic candidates who have lost their jobs due to the pandemic and have the skills you are looking for. Searching for talent doesn't take a break!

What are the soft skills that companies should be looking for in candidates?

Communication is the number one soft skill that businesses should be looking for in potential candidates. This may seem like a strange skill to really put the focus on, but in today's world, you want to know how candidates are actually communicating. For example, here are some things to look for and questions to ask, which will allow you to see their communication skills.

Things to look for:

- Do they seem to have a chip on their shoulder?
- Are they realistic?
- Are they listening? (Which is a part of communication)

Questions to ask:

- Can you describe your typical day?
- What does work-life balance mean to you?
- How do you handle the phone and phone calls?
- What kind of distractions do you have at home, and how do you deal with them?
- How do you feel about working remotely?

Be sure to watch a candidate's eyes and body language when interviewing.

"Body language is a very powerful tool. We had body language before we had speech, and apparently, 80 percent of what you understand in a conversation is read through the body, not the words." —Deborah Bull

With video interviews, you can still make eye contact and watch a person's body language, so be sure to keep that in mind when talking with prospective candidates.

What questions should you ask your candidates, and what questions should you be asking your current employees during this time?

It is now an employer's market again, but businesses need to be careful about who they hire—and asking good questions is the way to learn if a candidate is the right fit.

You can ask questions such as:

- Did you get laid off?
- Did you get furloughed? How long were you with the company?
- Why do you feel you were let go?

And again, watch what they say and how they say it.

Don't be afraid to be direct with your questions.

When it comes to your current employees, ask them heartfelt questions:

- What are you doing?
- What ideas do you have?
- How are you handling things?

You want to give them a voice in your business. Of course, if they don't have a voice, it may be time to let them go. And these conversations shouldn't be every day—but every few weeks for a few minutes. It lets your current employees know that you care about them and what's going on in their lives.

During this time, it's about trust. You have to have trust that your employees are doing their best, and you have to trust in yourself that you are asking the right questions of potential new employees.

Finding candidates who are a fit for your business and can work with your current employees will only strengthen your company. You will find that your business experiences an increase in productivity and engagement, less turnover, and is better able to deal with changes in the work environment as they come.

Three Action Steps

1. Continue recruiting if your business is in a position to hire employees.
2. Watch how a candidate communicates with you during an interview—including body language and listening skills.
3. Be direct with your questions of candidates and current employees to get the answers you need.

Connect with Jennifer Mastor at www.linkedin.com/in/mastor/

Hiring

Jennifer Mastor
Owner & Professional Recruiter
MASTOR Recruiting and Consulting

Jennifer represents companies of all sizes that need to hire front and back-end individuals. She recruits for entry-level to "C" Suite for all positions, with the exception of IT and medical roles. Additionally, she helps support individuals who need assistance with career decisions.

Main Takeaway

Candidates need to approach interviewing with the mindset of "What can I do to help and contribute?" to this business.

Questions

1. What do candidates need to ask when sitting in front of a potential employer?

2. What does the candidate's mindset need to be when interviewing?

3. What are some additional important questions that can be asked when interviewing?

Interview: What does every applicant need to know right now about hiring?

With the current conditions as they are, what do businesses need to know right now about recruiting? It's a topic that not only benefits businesses but benefits job applicants, too. Jennifer Mastor is a professional recruiter who represents companies of all sizes that need to hire front and back-end individuals. She also supports applicants as they make important career decisions. And there's no one better to help businesses and employment candidates during these times.

What do candidates need to ask when sitting in front of a potential employer?

Candidates need to ask a wide variety of questions nowadays.

But when it comes to the portion of the interview where the hiring manager says, "Do you have any questions for me?"—there's one question that I coach all of my clients to ask. And it's a question that I don't think gets asked often. The question is: How can I help and contribute? As soon as you ask that question, you have now set the tone of the interview—because now the employer knows that you are there for a reason. You have let the interviewer know that you are there to help them—not yourself.

Interviewing can be a stressful experience, especially if you are in need of a job or highly desire the role you are interviewing for. But if you can show that you are there to be an asset to the company, you will leave a positive impression on the hiring manager. And imagine what you are going to learn about the company by asking this question. It's definitely going to provide you insight into whether this is the right fit for you.

What does the candidate's mindset need to be when interviewing?

When you ask certain questions, your attitude and your tone really have to be, "What's in it for the employer,"—not yourself. The employer is making an investment in you, and they want to know if you are worth it. By asking certain questions, it's going to allow them to hear that you are here to make a positive contribution to the company. Not just to collect a paycheck. Not just to be a body Monday through Friday. But that you truly want to help a company grow—no matter what the role is.

Now your potential employer is going to look at you and think, "Wow! Okay . . . I'm not getting somebody who's going to ask me question after question about benefits, or salary, or promotions." Because questions about those topics are a signal of an entitled person. A person who's in it solely for them.

Hiring managers are looking for people that have the right personality and are a cultural fit for their business. Skills can be taught but personality cannot.

When you are in a job and feel like you are making positive contributions to the company and its growth, how does it make you feel? Like you are valued? Like you are an important part of the team? Then why wouldn't you want to start fostering that feeling at your initial interview?

What are some additional important questions that can be asked when interviewing?

High potential candidates need to express their curiosity and show that they are highly invested in learning more about the company and the roles within the company.

- What is the biggest opportunity for this role?
- What is the most challenging aspect of it? (This is because they want to know what you're walking into.)
- What does success in this position look like? (This is a really strong question to get some great dialogue going back and forth with either the hiring manager or the manager you are interviewing with as a first or final step of the hiring process.)
- Can you describe your team in three words? Why those three words?

And I think one of my favorite questions that anybody can ask is: How did the company determine its mission?

No matter what kind of position that you're interviewing for, you can ask:

- How is your training set up for remote workers?

- How do you like to communicate? (This is a question that I also have employers ask applicants. Because in today's world, if we're going to continue working like this, both the potential employee and the employer need to know that you can go back and forth on video. They need to know that you can text. They need to know that you can ask questions and get the answers you need with this type of communication.)

- Can you share the culture of the company with me, since I can't walk in and see it or feel it?

Then you can also ask a closing question, for example:

Is there anything that you don't see on my resume that you'd like to know about me? (This is a good question as it gives an employer permission to ask anything personal—which they're not allowed to do—and that's a really strong indication that you are highly interested in the role.)

Asking relevant questions about communication and showing that you are tech-savvy and have good communication skills—via a wide variety of platforms—allows you to show how you are a fit for the company and their culture during these times.

Three Action Steps

1. Approach interviews with the mindset of "How can I help you?" versus a "What's in it for me?" mentality.

2. Know that hiring managers are looking for people who have the right personality and are a cultural fit for their business.

3. Ask questions that show your curiosity about the business—especially in regard to communication.

Connect with Jennifer Mastor at www.linkedin.com/in/mastor/

Value Your People

Bob Graham
CEO
Breakthrough Solutions

Bob Graham, CEO of Breakthrough Solutions, coaches, trains, and researches how people interact with each other. He helps entrepreneurs and business leaders expand their businesses, build more effective teams, create more efficiency in their work and in their business, all by encouraging a better ROI on their biggest investment, which is their people.

Main Takeaway

Invest in your people to uncover huge gains in your company's creativity, innovation, and productivity.

Questions

1. How much value do companies really put into people?

2. What are the starting points for developing trust?

3. What else is needed for working with people?

Interview: What do businesses need to know right now about people?

There are bits and pieces that we're all missing in the midst of all of everything that's going on. I thought it would be helpful to bring in experts that could answer the question of what businesses need to know right now. Bob Graham was the first to say yes to participate.

How much value do companies really put in people? Are they paying attention to their people, and especially now?

Well, it's kind of funny. I would have said, historically, companies don't value their people the way they need to. But suddenly now, everyone's working from home. And that changes the paradigm. And I think companies are seeing the value of their people when things are not getting done or when things are being done differently. And they're starting to have to retool how those relationships are.

So, for instance, a lot of people in jobs complained to me about work-life balance. Suddenly when people were working at home, there's a necessity for work-life balance. If they have children, they're homeschooling because the schools are closed, and they have to deal with them in different ways. Companies are having to understand their employees better and also be more creative in how the technology works with their employees. They also need to consider how they manage employees. One of the unfortunate aspects of this pandemic is all of the company's weaknesses are highlighted. And we're seeing this over and over. Companies don't have really good processes and systems in place to manage people and to lead them, and now, these issues are starting to show up a lot in companies that I talked to.

In the past, I could see the person in the room across the hall. I knew what they were doing, but now, I don't know what they're doing. There's a trust factor. A lot of employers, a lot of managers, and leaders don't trust that their employees are actually working. As a recent study from Airtasker shows, people who work at home don't waste time on their daily commute, and they are more productive and have a healthier lifestyle, which translates into fewer health issues.

A lot of companies are going to see this as an amazing experiment in what's possible. And from a productivity standpoint and an effectiveness standpoint, this is amazing fuel for having businesses that don't have employees come in all the time. An employee might come in once or twice a week or once a month, depending on the position that they hold. Businesses could be saving tons on brick-and-mortar structures and the ancillary services that have to happen when you have a big building.

What I was seeing right before this pandemic was businesses were moving to open workspaces. In open workspaces, people didn't have the ability to prioritize and focus. Anyone could walk in. Your space wasn't your own. And I was thinking, "Oh my gosh, this, to me, is a recipe for disaster." But if we could blend that with having your deep workspace at home, I just think that would be rocket fuel. There's a lot of opportunity there.

One of the keys at the core of all these changes and a requirement to be effective in any kind of work environment with people is trust. You have to assume the best until they (or you) choose otherwise. Many employers and managers are fearful that they're being taken for a ride. In this new environment, there is a greater need for trust. That's a challenge in many workplaces, traditional or otherwise.

What are the starting points for developing trust?

The first thing is to get on a shared space in terms of what objectives are. Often trust is eroded when one or the other party doesn't know what to expect. A manager needs to sit down with the employee over a video call and decide:

- What is that person working on?
- What are the priorities?
- How do they fit into what I'm doing?

Set expectations for when something should be done in a shared environment.

I'm a big believer in shared responsibility and setting goals, and then having a manager or leader give ownership to the employee. The employee goes and does the task. How they get there is fine. If they need help—call, but do not micromanage. As a manager, do not say, "It's been two hours, what did you do?" That doesn't work. That's not the world that most people, especially people who are professionals, want.

Often in this climate, what I hear from employees is, "I was getting calls every two hours from my boss." I had one employee in a company say they had to give an hourly report by email about what they were doing and never got a confirmation that the supervisor even received it. That plan held up for three days, and the person wondered, "Why am I doing this?" It was busy work.

Trust. At the foundation of trust is good, clear, consistent communication. And communication goes back and forth. Both employee and manager need to know, "If I'm sending an email, I want the email response back." Trust is clarity in the next action. Set expectations of what is going to happen when the step is completed—from both sides. If the manager is participating and if the employee is participating, what does a good solution or good outcome look like for both of them? Having good, clear communication with next step actions.

What else is needed for working with people?

Organizations need to look at a shared vision. Leading and being led is easier when you have a shared vision. This is not "Do this because . . ." but "Do this because we are trying to achieve X." Communicate to your employees their role as part of getting to X. People like to be on a quest. Even the lowest level employee in an organization can be part of that quest if they understand the role, even the person that cleans the building. You may think, "Oh, that person should know." The reality is they don't. Imagine if the cleaning person understood, along with everyone working, that cleaning of the building means that when people can come back, they are going to see an inviting environment that makes them feel better about our company, which makes them more apt to want to share with us and buy from us. "Oh, wow!" they think. When we start looking at it from that perspective, we have a shared vision, which is a big part of communication.

"Belonging" is the number one reason why people stay at a job or

move on. The Harvard Business Review found that 40 percent of people say that they feel isolated at work, which causes less commitment and engagement and more departing for other jobs. If you can foster that sense of belonging with your people by providing a place that they feel like they contribute, that they're trusted, that they're valued as a human being, and they're part of a greater whole, you've hit the magic sauce. If your company isn't feeling like you're in that magic space yet, I would invite you to reach out to Bob.

Three Action Steps

1. Be creative and use the challenges you are facing as an opportunity to try something new. A blend of your current solution and the new one you are creating could be the rocket fuel to move your business forward.

2. Use clear communication and expectations to build trust.

3. Develop and share a "shared vision" with every person in your organization.

Connect with Bob Graham at BreakthroughSolutions.co and www.linkedin.com/in/bob-graham/

Business & Mental Health

Fred Chanteau
CEO
Affiliated Santé Group

Fred has been involved in the area of behavioral health for over 40 years. He is the CEO of the Affiliated Santé Group, which serves everyday people who are experiencing a significant crisis in their lives or the lives of their loved ones. The company provides mobile crisis teams staffed with licensed clinicians to meet with individuals in crisis at their homes or other locations. The company works closely with law enforcement in response to 911 calls as well as other first responders. They also provide urgent psychiatric care for individuals who may need to be seen by a psychiatrist within 24 hours. The Santé Group serves 60 percent of Maryland counties, as well as Mecklenburg County and the city of Charlotte, North Carolina.

Main Takeaway

During times of crisis, it's essential that you reach out to your staff and check on their mental well-being—especially if they are working from home/telecommuting as you might not have that daily face-to-face interaction with them.

Questions

1. What are Crisis Response services?

2. What have you seen change over the last year about crisis services?

3. What should businesses and business owners know about mental health and behavioral health crisis services? What could they be doing with their own employees or with their loved ones?

4. Have you seen an increased need for adolescents and teens due to isolation?

Interview: What do businesses need to know right now about behavioral health?

Fred Chanteau is the CEO of the Affiliated Santé Group, which serves everyday people who are experiencing a significant crisis in their lives or the lives of their loved ones. The company provides mobile crisis teams staffed with licensed clinicians to meet with individuals in cases at their homes or other locations. They work closely with law enforcement in response to 911 calls as well as for first responders. And they provide urgent psychiatric care for individuals who may need to be seen by psychiatrists within 24 hours. Having been involved in the area of behavioral health for over 40 years, he's the ideal person to share what businesses need to know right now about behavioral health.

What are Crisis Response services?

We have a broad range of trained clinicians with degrees and licenses, and they are literally Mental Health First Responders. We are basically on-demand responders, to folks at home, in the community, to the police, really anywhere that a crisis may occur for someone.

And we all define those crises differently. So, I can't tell you that all of our crises are related to mental health, or all of them are suicide cases. They all vary. You define it the way you want.

But essentially, we get a call, and we assess that call. And if need be, we send people out into the community in vehicles to meet with those folks who try to resolve things as quickly as we can. It's really kind of mental health work where the rubber meets the road.

What have you seen change over the last year about crisis services?

It was interesting. Initially, in April, May, and maybe the beginning of June, our calls actually went down. And that kind of made sense. People were afraid to come into contact with folks.

But in July and August, they really surged from what we were seeing. A lot of folks were feeling isolated, depressed, and suicidal. The number of suicides has really kind of blown up. Domestic violence has increased tremendously. So, those things all of a sudden began to finally percolate as folks had been by themselves with a tight crew for a really long time.

And we're afraid of losing jobs or have lost jobs. It reflects a lot of what happened during the recession in 2009. People just started panicking.

Statistical evidence of increased depression, suicides, and instances of domestic violence during the quarantine are beginning to be released, but it's not surprising to know that we experienced increases in these things during these stressful times.

What should businesses and business owners know about mental health and behavioral health crisis services? What could they be doing with their own employees or with their loved ones?

Every business is going to be a little different. But I think the most important thing is to remain vigilant with your folks, especially now that they are telecommuting. You don't have the ability necessarily to touch base with them and see a sad face, or maybe they're not talking as often. I think contacting them and being vigilant about how they show up, touching base with people, and asking, "How are you doing?" is essential. And that way, maybe you have the opportunity to fend off what may or may not be going on with them.

The change in work, going from the office to working at home alone, can affect your well-being. For some, it's no big deal; they really enjoy working alone. But for others, it might be important to create an environment where there is a sense of community.

Reach out to people as much as possible. We've been struggling with that, as I'm sure a lot of companies have.

And so, we have turned to town hall meetings as opportunities to share. We've expanded our wellness activities to where we have online games with folks where they can join, or yoga, and I'm sure a lot of other folks are doing that kind of thing. And it really does appeal to a set of staff, and they're able to utilize that. Others just really love telecommuting and don't need anything.

Some employees say, "Hey, I wish I never had to come back. This is totally wonderful." And then others are just saying, "I can't work by myself anymore. Can I come back in?"

For me, this has been a tough time because I like working with groups. I get energy from groups. I get creativity from them. And so, I have found it more difficult to remain productive and happy working and telecommuting. So, I try to call a lot of folks. I try to Zoom with a lot of people—because seeing their faces, I think, is more important than just talking to them on the phone.

Have you reached out to your employees to see how they're doing with working from home? Are they thriving, or do they miss the camaraderie and community atmosphere that the office brought to them?

Have you seen an increased need for adolescents and teens due to the isolation?

Yes, there has been an uptick in that. There has been an uptick in individual suicidology with teens. The use of text and chat lines, while we don't offer them, have really expanded, and they've noticed an increase in volume. Part of it has also to do with the fact that they're spending so much time with their parents, and they don't have those relationships outside of the family where they usually talk about things.

Three Action Steps

1. Remain vigilant with your employees and check in with them often to know how they are doing during times of stress

2. Recognize that some may be handling working from home well, while others are struggling with the isolation.

3. Encourage your employees to communicate with you and coworkers as they need to.

Connect with Fred Chanteau at
www.linkedin.com/in/fred-chanteau-aa185b1b/ or
www.thesantegroup.org/contact-us

DIVERSITY, INCLUSION, EQUITY & BELONGINGNESS

Embrace Diversity to Build a Better Workplace | 199

with Aparajita Jeedigunta

Be Interested and Listen | 204

with Kachelle Kelly

Be Willing to Converse | 209

with Dr. Rochelin Herold

Creating a Safe Space for Conversation | 216

with Bob Graham

DIVERSITY, INCLUSION, EQUITY & BELONGINGNESS

None of us, including me, ever do great things. But we can all do small things, with great love, and together we can do something wonderful.

—Mother Teresa

A shift towards awareness of diversity, inclusion, equity, and belongingness means that we have the opportunity to tap into the brilliance of each person to make our world a better place. Our time in isolation during the pandemic only solidified the importance of community and belonging. These next interviews came in response to the unrest in the United States due to social injustice. Diversity is not about seeing each other as different and less than, but instead that we are each uniquely suited to be part of "Team Human," to do great things together. Most importantly, engage from an authentic desire to improve our world and not just to be seen on the "right" side of an issue.

Aparajita Jeedigunta of AJ Rao, LLC emphasizes the importance of diversity and inclusion to business growth. Your strength as a business is in your people and in your ability to tap into the unique knowledge and experience that each person brings.

Kachelle Kelly of Kachelle Kelly International, Inc continues the conversation exploring what else businesses are doing or need to do to address social injustice. At the center of what is needed is greater listening and then a step towards action.

Dr. Rochelin Herold of Maryland Spine Institute Integrative Healthcare shares the impact of the protests in the United States. He talks about where and how to open up conversations about difficult topics.

Bob Graham of Breakthrough Solutions shares how to be intentional about engagement and when partaking in controversial topics makes sense from a business perspective.

Embrace Diversity to Build a Better Workplace

Aparajita Jeedigunta
PhD, CPEC, ACP, Diversity, Equity & Inclusion Leader and
Strategist
AJ Rao, LLC

Dr. AJ Jeedigunta helps bridge the gap between business health and success and employee well-being and success. She helps ambitious working professionals transform themselves into authentic, intentional, visible leaders who are seen, heard, valued, and recognized. She helps companies increase their profits by creating intentionally inclusive cultures where their visible leaders can thrive.

Main Takeaway

Belongingness in the workplace is about recognizing and embracing people's differences and respecting and valuing the unique perspectives that people bring.

Questions

1. What do diversity, equity, inclusion, and belongingness have to do with business?

2. What does belongingness mean as a business owner?

3. Why is it harmful for businesses to participate in performative allyship as opposed to authentic allyship, and how can we as businesses make sure that we're being intentionally inclusive?

Interview: What do businesses need to know right now about belonging?

Dr. AJ Jeedigunta is a personality psychologist and Certified Professional Executive Coach. She's also a published author, podcaster, and traumatic brain injury survivor turned mental well-being advocate. She's a very well-rounded individual entrepreneur, and she's sharing what businesses need to know right now about belongingness.

What do diversity, equity, inclusion, and belongingness have to do with business?

Part of it is everything that's going on in our country right now; 2020 has run us through the wringer so many times over and in so many ways. But it's also made visible all of these things that we've been sweeping under the rug for 450 years, but really the last few decades as well.

This is important for businesses because as we look at population trends in America, we are going to a state where the majority of the future workforce, the future consumers, and customers—all of them don't identify as white. So, with that being said, if you are not including their perspectives, and if you're not giving them access to services, products, and experiences in an equitable way—in which they feel like they belong—you're really losing out on a lot of profit from the consumer perspective.

You're also losing out if you don't think about diversity, equity, inclusion, and belongingness. And, I add all four of those because right now, we're still focused on diversity numbers. We have to get past that. The workforce that you are going to have as a business owner, the talent that you would leave on the table by not creating equity, inclusion, and intentional inclusion and belonging, is really going to hurt your business. This is the only way your business is going to sustain itself into the future and actually have a chance of being profitable.

A sense of belonging is the number one reason why somebody will stay or leave their place of employment. And so many times, as business owners, we imagine that if we pay them more, if we give them more training, or provide recognition—which is important— we think that will be enough to make them stay. But really, people need to feel like they belong at their jobs.

What does belongingness mean as a business owner?

That is such a great question, and it goes back to a fundamental human need. This need to belong is the origin of social psychology as a whole field. We know that this need to belong is universal, and what that really means is that somebody you know, a particular person, an individual—they feel like they belong if they are able to include themselves and be included in conversations, in decisions, in the informal, unspoken norms and etiquettes and accompany all of those because of their uniqueness, not despite it.
That's where the belongingness aspect comes in.

Now what we know now is that 61 percent of the US workforce actually covers or hides essential aspects of themselves because they feel like they're going to be thought about negatively, they're going to be judged, or they're going to be criticized, and that's especially salient in moments of feedback and conflict resolution. They just shut down. So, they are not able to bring their whole selves to the situation and thrive and be able to participate, be able to be seen, heard, valued and appreciated, and recognized because of their unique journey.

That's what belongingness is about. It is that I recognize that you are different. I recognize your differences, and I embrace them. I respect them, and I value you because you bring in a unique perspective.

If people showed up as their whole self, what's possible? If you know intimately about the things that your employer is talking about in the market that they want to reach, and you know about that because of your personal experience, and you can share—how much more valuable would someone be to an employer? And how valuable would it be as an employer to have a workforce of people who feel like they can contribute with their whole selves.

Why is it harmful for businesses to participate in performative allyship as opposed to authentic allyship, and how can we as businesses make sure that we're being intentionally inclusive?

The big harm with performative allyship is that it actually erodes trust. If all you're doing is just talking the talk, and you're taking advantage of the moments where you can sort of slip a few words in and then sit back and relax, people notice that—especially in this day and age of social media and with information being so rapidly disseminated.

People notice when you don't have real deliverables and when you don't have real actions. I think our mutual friend, Ruthie Bowles, actually did a great post about that with the Stitch Fix statement. So, something like that, where you don't have things that you hold yourself accountable for or other people can hold you accountable for, immediately erodes trust.

And consumers are becoming more and more socially and societally conscientious. As this movement is happening, it's very easy to recognize performative allyship because you'll see one or two posts on them, and then there's nothing.

If the companies that you're working with or if your company only made the big blanket statement that every single company provided a month ago, and you've done nothing else, then it may be time to look in the mirror and ask yourself some deeper questions.

Three Action Steps

1. Think about diversity, equity, inclusion, and belongingness because without doing so, you risk leaving talent on the table and hurting your business.

2. Recognize, embrace, value, and respect the unique perspectives that people can bring to you and your business.

3. Participate in authentic allyship so that you don't erode trust.

Connect with Dr Aparajita Jeedigunta at
www.linkedin.com/in/aparajitajeedigunta

Be Interested and Listen

Kachelle Kelly
DEI, EQ & Leadership Trainer, Author & Speaker
Kachelle Kelly International, Inc.

Kachelle Kelly is a five-time author, including a women's, men's, and children's prayer guide for entrepreneurs, keynote speaker, and corporate trainer. She trains on topics such as leadership skills for women, effective communication, dealing with difficult people, and emotional intelligence. She also recently launched an online course, "A New Journey for Non-Blacks: Becoming Anti-Racist & Effective Allies for the Black Community."

Main Takeaway

Conversations need to be had so that the white community truly understands the history of the Black community and can become anti-racist and effective allies.

Questions

1. What inspired you to create your new online program, "A New Journey for Non-Blacks"?

2. What do you see as some of the steps that need to be taken so that we don't lose energy and can create a new landscape?

3. How can we tell the story of different communities, for example, immigrants or women or people of color?

Interview: What do businesses need to know right now about being anti-racist?

Kachelle Kelly is a five-time author, a keynote speaker, and a corporate trainer. She trains on topics such as leadership skills for women, effective communication, dealing with difficult people, and emotional intelligence. She's launched a new course entitled, "A New Journey for Non-Blacks: Becoming Anti-Racist & Effective Allies for the Black Community," and she's sharing what businesses need to know right now about being anti-racist.

What inspired you to create your new online program, "A New Journey for Non-Blacks: Becoming Anti-Racist and Effective Allies for the Black Community"?

The current climate.

So, George Floyd happened. And from there, I saw a lot of scrambling. And it was very interesting. I think because people got to actually see it happen (the killing of George Floyd) is why the outrage happened. Because as a Black community, we've experienced this. We experience it every year, a couple of times during a year.

But because the outrage was so alarming, and then I don't even know why white people got in the conversation all of a sudden, but everybody started looking at companies to see what their response was. So, I don't know how we got there, but we're here.

And everybody is very, very careful about who they're doing business with, and they're canceling business relationships right now if you have not responded in a way to say, "Are you anti-racist?"

I think a lot of times, people will say, "I'm not racist. I'm not racist. I don't have a racist bone in my body. I have Black friends." But the real test is, are you anti-racist without being friends? If you've been around your white friends or white colleagues, and they've said something racist, did you say something? What side of history are you going to be on? And that's what I think it is important that people understand the difference between not racist to anti-racist.

I saw a lot of scrambling with companies. They said, "I've got to get with my team, and we've got to put something out there. And we've got to put up this black square. We've got to put up 'I can't breathe' memes, and we've got to say that we don't like this."

Then I saw a lot of coaching groups that I was a part of, and in these groups, there was a lot of bickering between people. It was like a racial war going on in these groups. There were thousands of people, and they were saying, "Okay, listen, this thing is going on. You are the person that brought us all together, and we've paid you $10 to $20,000 for this coaching program, and we don't feel included in this program. What's up?" And they didn't know how to handle it as a company because they had said, we don't talk about religion. We don't talk about politics. We don't talk about racism. We never have.

But in times of pain—it's different, and the conversation needs to be had. So, I need for businesses to understand that we are in a new norm right now. And the way that we used to do things in the past is no longer acceptable.

And you can check your inbox, check your email, and you've probably gotten an email from every person you've ever done business with—every airline, your cable provider, every single company—everyone has been in a flurry to come out with a diversity plan. And that's where we're at.

I wrote the course because I saw all of those people doing those things, and now the flurry is gone. Now it's time to do the work. Now it's time to actually learn the history of Black people. Now it's time not just to do things right, but to learn how we got here and learn those things that they don't even teach in history books or history schools, all this history that we know as Black people. But you cannot be our allies and love us and support us if you don't know us.

The initial flurry has passed, and most companies have made a statement. But what are you doing now?

What do you see as some of the steps that need to be taken so that we don't lose energy and can create a new landscape?

Your work needs to happen, and it's not sending out a book list, which a lot of companies are doing. It's about talking to your Black employees. It's about talking to your Black clients and saying, "You know, maybe having focus groups with the people that are in your group is needed." And asking, "How can I serve you better? What is missing from this organization that I could have overlooked?" Because you don't know what you don't know.

The thing about it is that you've got to sit down and have the conversation not given to the NAACP. You've got Black customers right here to talk to. We are open. We are willing. We want to talk to you and tell you.

Every coaching group that I'm in, it's always the Black subgroup that people create because they don't feel included in the big group, and that should stop because everybody paid the same; it's the same opportunity. Putting more Black people on your podcasts and on your stages. I've gone to conferences and paid $20,000 and $5,000, and I've never even seen a Black person on stage, or even as an intern checking people in.

Are you excited for the conversation? You should be. This is an opportunity to really address things that we haven't addressed as a country. There are different stories to be told, and now is the time to hear them.

How can we tell the story of different communities, for example, immigrants or women or people of color?

My parents, when they were 23 and 24 years old, could not drink from a fountain. And so, I think the misconception is that we talk about slavery and say, "It was 400 years ago." But my grandfather was a slave. He picked cotton and lived in my parents' house until he died. So, it's not as far removed as people think.

Be interested and listen to people. Because everybody is trying to fit in with white people, that's just our view—that we're trying to do everything to be accepted. When, if you really think about it, and you call a spade a spade, it's like no one is ever interested in who we are. And it's always like this meme that says, "The people love our culture, but they hate us."

The conversation needs to be had because we never thought we had the opportunity to say things like that and for people to listen. And, at the moment, it may hurt, and you may say, "I have been pretty crappy for not even wanting to listen to things like this. But I want to know now." The conversation needs to be had.

Have you had conversations with your Black employees and clients to see how you can serve them better? And more importantly, have you listened to what they've had to say?

Three Action Steps

1. Know that the way of doing things in the past is no longer acceptable, and tough conversations need to be had about subjects such as race and racism.

2. Ask questions of your Black employees and customers to see how you can serve them better.

3. Be interested and willing to listen to the conversations that are happening regarding race and racism.

Connect with Kachelle Kelly
at www.linkedin.com/in/kachellekelly/ or www.kachellekelly.com

Be Willing to Converse

Dr. Rochelin Herold
Owner/Clinical Director at MSI Integrative Healthcare
MSI Integrative Healthcare

Dr. Roch Herold is the founder, clinical director, and owner of the Maryland Spine Institute (MSI) Integrative Healthcare. He studied at the University of West Virginia University, and he's a chiropractor with physical therapy privileges. As a business owner, he is constantly continuing his education and putting his patients first in order to incorporate modern practices and be a mentor and leader in health and wellness.

Main Takeaway

Don't be afraid to have the difficult conversations with your employees and clients because it's important to recognize that these are human beings first—and they are affected by what is happening in the world.

Question

1. As a business owner, how do you bring these conversations into your work? And what changes do you think need to be made for businesses to address—or not address—these things?

Interview: What do businesses need to know right now about the protests and the impact it is having on business owners?

Dr. Roch Herold is the founder, clinical director, and owner of the Maryland Spine Institute. He's a chiropractor with physical therapy privileges. He studied at the University of West Virginia University. He's a busy dad and business owner, and he is constantly continuing his education and putting his patients first in order to bring modern practices and be a mentor and leader in health and wellness.

Dr. Herold is sharing what businesses need to know right now about the protests and the impact it's having on business owners. As a Black, Haitian-American, and owner of a business, he's the perfect person to engage with in this conversation.

We thought that COVID-19 was going to be the worst of what we had to endure in 2020, and then a video surfaced of a man named George Floyd. And we find ourselves asking how a 911 call for a counterfeit bill led to somebody dying on the streets of Minneapolis at the hands of a police officer.

It was stated that it was standard protocol for the store to call 911 for the counterfeit bill. I think where the injustice and outrage came from is that people wondered where was the standard protocol for the police officers in apprehending and dealing with Mr. Floyd? That's where the outrage came from.

The fact is that he was unable to breathe properly for eight-plus minutes, and you find yourself asking, "How did this happen?" He didn't look different than anyone else—other than being an African American person. And he died. As a father, I'm thinking, "Man, you know what? This could be me. This could be my son or my daughter."

This is also coming on the heels of Ahmaud Arbery, who was a young man that was shot down in Georgia, and then Breonna Taylor, who was a young lady that was a civil servant and was killed in her own home. And these things have been happening over the past few years. We all remember Trayvon Martin. In Baltimore, there was Freddie Gray.

Within the African American community, we find ourselves asking, "When is enough? When are we going to change the policies?" Of course, you can't really legislate good thinking. If somebody has been raised to think differently about somebody, you can't legislate that out of them; you can't get rid of systemic racism. But you can put some policies in place to protect oppressed people.

You can't take out the systemic racism from people who have learned it from generation to generation, and that's what they grew up with. But you can do things to protect a class of people who have been consistently and constantly oppressed and done so with public policy and with ignorance.

As a business owner, how do you bring these conversations into your work? And what changes do you think need to be made for businesses to address—or not address—these things?

I was telling you earlier that you actually had a really good segment with Bob Graham. He said you have two scenarios. You can say that the business is not going to take any stance, so that you don't alienate any clientele or staff members that might be working with you. And the alternative is to at least create a safe space so that at least you address it, and you address the elephant in the room and create a safe space for your employees and staff members so they can talk about it. This allows your employees to feel free to openly discuss and talk about the current situation without judgment and without malice.

Our company, MSI, we have at least done the latter. We have at least addressed it in an office meeting. Whenever there is any unrest or anything socially going on, we'll bring it up. We do know that it does cause some tension in the office environment. It does cause stress, and it does cause people to react differently in the moment. Sometimes in our office meetings, we just want to clear the air, and we say, "Hey, look, we know this is going on. If anybody wants to talk about it, or if there's anything that we can do to help anybody, whether it's on the mental health side of it, or whether it's anything that we can do to talk about it and address it—let us know." I think that is something that shows the employees that they're valuable to me not just as an employee—but as a human being who has feelings.

It's not just your employees who are dealing with these things; it's your clientele also. They will see that you're willing to open up these conversations, to hear the voices that, perhaps, have not been heard, and to be willing to accept that there are feelings that come along with this, and it's not okay just to pretend that it doesn't exist.

Somebody said, "You know it's not like there is that much more racism going on right now. It's just being recorded more." And I think that with Facebook and people sharing their feelings and this and that, things are just coming more to life. You know, the chickens are coming home to roost. If we're all going to live in this world together, then we're going to have to create these spaces to deal with them.

I'm remembering back to the civil rights movement, where you really didn't see a lot of white America taking part in the marches. It was mostly the Black people in Birmingham and the bus boycott. But it was when Bloody Sunday happened, when now-Congressman John Lewis, along with countless others, were marching across the bridge peacefully, and they were beaten and attacked by police. It was recorded for the world to see.

And it was around that time that King also wrote a letter from the Birmingham jail, which I encourage everybody to read, because Dr. Martin Luther King was writing to the white clergyman that were telling him that now is really not the time to protest and now is really not the time to march. They said he was becoming an agitator and that he was trying to disrupt things. The white clergy said that we have a peaceful society, a law-and-order society, and asked Dr. King why he was messing things up?

In his letter, which again, I encourage everybody to read because it's a very long letter, but it's very impactful, he asks, "When is the right time to protest?"

So often, the Negroes have heard, "Wait." And wait has been synonymous with never when it comes to when is a good time to protest.[2]

---

2 — Dr. Rochelin Herold is paraphrasing from Dr. Martin Luther King, Jr's, "Letter from a Birmingham Jail" which states, "For years now I have heard the word 'Wait!' It rings in the ear of every Negro with piercing familiarity. This "Wait" has almost always meant 'Never.'"

With the NFL not too long ago, there was a peaceful protest by Colin Kaepernick, which drew different sides on Facebook, and whether you agreed with what he did, he was still doing it peacefully. Now you see certain football players calling out certain teams because they're like, "Hey, wait a minute. Now you're with us and talking about the blackout because the streets are burning and all of this stuff." Well, when somebody was trying to do it peacefully, they said it was about the flag. They said it was about all these other things when the very person that protested said it was about police brutality.

There is no one right way to protest that's going to make everybody comfortable. I definitely do not agree with the violence and the looting. I do think that there are other outside agitators that are trying to corrupt the message that people are trying to do with their peaceful protests. But we have to look beyond that we and we have to call that out as well.

I do want to take my time to say that my best friend is a police officer. He's in the first precinct in New York City, which is going crazy right now as well. I have countless patients who are police officers, and to peacefully protest does not mean that you're against police. To peacefully protest and to demand justice for not just George Floyd, but to say, "Let's change the policies so that those that are crossing the line are held accountable," is not being against the police.

Let's also celebrate the police because they have a heck of a hard time trying to bear the burdens of society. I feel like too many times when there's something wrong with society; we want the police to fix it. But it's not a police officer's job to fix everything wrong with education. It's not a police officer's job to fix everything wrong in society. When things blow up like this, they're looked at as the antagonist. And I do want to take this time to say, "No, it's not all police officers." The majority of people in law enforcement are doing the right thing, and they are walking with the protesters, and they are doing what they have to do to make sure that the communities in which they serve know that they have their back.

But what do we do when things go too far and certain people cross the line? How do we protect not just African Americans but all citizens, and I think that's where the conversation is going.

That's why the world is waking up, and this is really a fight for humanity because no one person should die on the streets while being apprehended.

I'll end with a story. I told you I was Haitian American, and my parents came here because there was a lot of political persecution in Haiti. One time, I was maybe 11, 12 years old, I came home, and my grandmother, who was very strong, probably one of the strongest women that I know, was crying profusely. I said, "Man, what's wrong with her? Why is she crying?" And she was saying, "Oh, they killed Claudie. They killed Claudie." My mother had a cousin named Claudie, and because the government was unchecked, it got so corrupt that the dictator and the political class had their own secret police—kind of like a Gestapo. Those individuals who were corrupt police officers, they basically beat one of my cousins because he had a radio show that was talking about the government and talking about mobilizing; he wasn't really talking bad, but about he was just trying to mobilize and trying to get laws passed, and they killed him. They brutally murdered him. And at that time, I said, "Wow! Well, I'm glad that's only happening in Haiti, and I'm glad that's not happening in America."

And now, as I've grown up, and I see stories unfolding, it's happening in America. We're better than this. We are the city on a hill. We are the beacon of light that all other countries want to come to. But if we want to live up to our values that every man is created equal and that every man can pursue life, liberty, and happiness, then we have to be able to have these conversations. And we have to be able to not only have these conversations but to demand justice. Because a lot of times the freedom is not given, it usually has to be demanded by the oppressor. That's where we are right now. And I think we can do it peacefully.

But we can also engage the community so that we can increase voter turnout. And we can engage communities so that we start reducing all the other issues that we have in Black America— such as housing prices, drugs in the community, and education. But right now, the light is shining on the criminal justice system.

Some things I would encourage everybody to read that letter from the Birmingham Jail. There's a great Netflix movie that talks about the criminal justice system called *13th* on Netflix, and if you haven't watched that, I would definitely watch that. There are groups in Baltimore that are trying to not just work together with the police, but also trying to reduce the violence that's going on within the community. There's one that's called We Are Us, and it's a bunch of men from all different faiths and backgrounds, and they walk the streets of Baltimore, and they're talking to the young kids and trying to show them that there's a better way. There are plenty of things going on. It may not be on CNN, Fox News, and MSNBC, but they're happening. That's what I think your community, meaning basically white America, should see—and not just look at what's on the news, but really talk to people, open up the conversation and talk to people that are doing things in a positive way to improve the community, then we're going to go a whole lot further than just seeing riots on TV.

Three Action Steps

1. Allow your employees to feel free to openly discuss and talk about current situations without judgment and without malice.

2. Recognize that people may feel stressed or react differently in the moment based on the current situation.

3. Be willing to open up conversations with people that may not have had their voices heard.

Connect with Dr. Herold at
www.linkedin.com/in/rochelin-herold-dc-10802440/

Creating a Safe Space for Conversation

Bob Graham
CEO
Breakthrough Solutions

Bob Graham, CEO of Breakthrough Solutions, coaches, trains, and researches how people interact with each other. He helps entrepreneurs and business leaders expand their businesses, build more effective teams, and create more efficiency in their work and in their business, all by encouraging a better ROI on their biggest investment, which is their people.

Main Takeaway

Decide if you help or hinder your business by becoming a part of the conversation. Additionally, because of the close relationship you have with clients and customers, consider being a safe space for them to have a conversation without sharing your opinion.

Question

1. What do businesses need to know right now about talking about controversial issues, or do you not talk about them at all?

Interview: What business owners need to know about talking about controversial issues.

Bob Graham, CEO of Breakthrough Solutions, coaches, trains, and researches how people interact with each other. He helps entrepreneurs and business leaders expand their businesses, build more effective teams, and create more efficiency in their work and in their business, all by encouraging a better ROI on their biggest investment, which is their people.

Bob is sharing what businesses need to know right now about talking about controversial issues. You probably have wondered whether you should talk about them or whether you should remain quiet. Bob, with his work on understanding and hearing people, is the perfect resource for helping us navigate the questions we have.

As a business owner, do we talk about the controversial issues? Or do we leave it off the table?

I need to have a couple of caveats for this discussion so that I can sleep well. I do not want to discuss any political views, social views, or economic views. This discussion we're having has no bearing on how anyone believes. I'm not espousing any point of view. I'm not discouraging any point of view. I'm being agnostic to all those things out there.

Where I would start the discussion with you is, does it make sense for you to add your voice to the chorus? If you are the owner of a business, if you are a key employee in a business, even if you're a line worker, what could happen with your customers? Because when I think about my business, my number one goal is to serve my customers. Does my viewpoint about this issue help in any way my customers?

You're the first person that I've talked to about this. We talked about where we were politically beforehand, and you gave me a very impassioned point of view. I provoked you with a couple of questions. But you learned that I do not bring politics into the conversation. In our beforehand discussion, you did not learn what my beliefs are on this issue.

I come from a background as a journalist, where you couldn't have a point of view. I was trained to put my perspective aside. So, I've had that blessing or curse. You can see it both ways. But I've taken that to my business. Because what I believe about this issue probably doesn't have any relevance to what I do with people.

Where it does have relevance, though, is that I know it's on people's minds. For example, if I'm doing an offering this week and we didn't have the results we expected, then I'm smart enough to realize that people are focused on these issues outside of work. And so, we have to be aware of what's going on in the world.

But I'm not a big believer that every company should make a statement about every social issue. Now, if it's an issue directly affecting you, you might make a statement. For instance, my company might make a statement about a first amendment issue. If Facebook were being clamped down on, I might make a statement about that because that affects my business.

Now, the other thing I would say is there's an alternative—and a very important alternative. One of the things I think people need more than ever before in our world is a safe place to have a discussion. And so, when you started to talk about this issue, my first reaction was, "Oh, don't want to go there. Don't want to go there." But I've learned that giving a person a place of safety so that they can share their point of view is a gift.

That doesn't mean I have to give you my point of view. I let you talk for three to four minutes about the issues. I did bring up a couple of issues with you. But if you think about what I brought up, I brought up like, New York Times headlines. I didn't give you my perspective; I made you feel safe so that you could share with me. Our customers want that, and they need that, especially if you have a close relationship with someone. This is a chance where they may not have a safe forum to explore their ideas.

Most of us are trying to figure out what we know, what we understand, and what we're thinking. And so, when someone, someone starts to share that with us, that's really valuable. They need that space. I'm always willing to let my clients and my customers share their perspectives, but I will not argue with them, and I will not give the slightest hint of what I believe—even if they really push me.

And it's funny because I have clients who say, "Why you've got to be a hardcore Republican," while others think I'm a hardcore liberal. The reason this is the case is that I can sit and listen to them on both sides of the aisle. I haven't given anything, and if I don't give them exactly what I believe, whether I agree or disagree, they assume that I align with them. And does it really matter if someone assumes that I align with them? That only emboldens our relationship. I haven't lied to them. I haven't misled them, and more importantly, I've given them that place of safety where they can think about and talk out some of the issues.

What is largely missing is actual real conversation, rather than just throwing out talking points, headlines, and bullet points. To be able to get to a point where you can freely share information back and forth is key. It's about hearing people. It's critical to understand that there are individuals in the conversations and that their background, their understandings, and their experiences are going to color everything that's going on.

I've had people who will start with one point of view when they start talking to me. I will give them that safe space, and they will discuss it with themselves. I might ask them a question, such as "Well, is that really true?" or "That's inconsistent with what I've been reading." And, in the course of that discussion, the person changed their point of view. I did not lobby them. I did not try to influence them. I tried to help them clarify their point of view because they felt comfortable enough to bring it up with me. And in homes where one member of the house believes certain things, and another member of the house believes other things, and they are at odds, the safe places are even more valuable.

Ultimately, we buy from people we know, like, and trust. When you shared your opinions earlier with me. My first thought was, "Man, I've gotten to a place with Nettie where she trusts me with the most valuable thing that she can have, which is her opinion." Because when you put your opinion out there, you run the risk of someone saying, "Whoa, you're a liar," or

"That's wrong," or "I refuse to be involved with you because of that opinion." And that doesn't help anyone.

We have crises all the time. If we took a stand on things every time a crisis arose, it would damage our business.

My thought is when you come to me for coaching, or when you come to me for training or to speak to your organization, you come to me because I know people. You do not come to me because I know about famine in Ethiopia. You do not come to me to talk about first amendment issues involving China. You come to me because I have a very specific set of skills.

Now, if there's a political issue that involves people—yes, I would have the discussion. So, if you want my views on millennials working in the workforce, absolutely. I'll talk all day about that—if you want it. If you want me to talk about how colleges do or don't prepare students to work in the world, you will get a very impassioned argument from me because those are in my wheelhouse in my business. But you will not get me talking about the things outside of that. I will not talk about sexual harassment policies.

I challenged Bob a little on whether sexual harassment is or is not a people issue.

It is a people issue, but I do not believe that a middle-aged white guy should be the person talking about that issue. If you want to talk about that issue, if you came to my company and wanted me to do something, I would point you in the direction of people who are far more gifted, who have a far better perspective than mine, because the perspective of the white male has dominated and I don't want to be aligned with that group—even if that's not my perspective. I do not feel that I'm qualified on that subject. Just like if someone comes to me and wants to be coached on how to lose weight. I coach people, but I don't know how to do that. I don't know how to train someone in sports. I certainly don't know how to train you in music, so I know what my lane is—and I stay in my lane. There's plenty for me to do in my lane. I would encourage people to think about what lane they are in. Because what happens is you have the person who's in eight lanes—and they are going nowhere.

It's important to remember that it's not about you as a person not caring about these issues. It's about being able to create a safe space, have a conversation, further the work that you're doing, be helpful with the skills you have, and not to contribute where you can't affect meaningful change.

The tire repair company should not be doing oil changes. That's not what they do. A company that does moving shouldn't be telling people how to avoid hoarding. Stay in your lane.

I always go back to, "What do my customers need from me? What do they expect from me when they write that check to me at the end of the month?" It is very, very rare for me to share an opinion about a current event. I just don't do it. I've trained myself because I don't want to get into a fight with someone about these issues. That doesn't help further things. What I often do, because I know the issues, I will provoke a person to think about their thoughts more broadly.

Finally, I'd like to share one more thing. I was involved with a company a couple of months ago that had a bad case of ransomware. It was an IT company, so they were managing people's technology. They chose to be very open and candid about it throughout the whole process. They sent an email out that day. They sent updates saying, "We're talking to the FBI." They were very open about something that most IT companies would choose not to share other than the mandatory things. Every time their sales director walks in the room, someone will say to them, "David, that was so awesome—how you kept us informed the whole way." There is a place to talk about things, especially when there's an elephant in the room.

If something is going on that affects your business, you've got to talk about it. I wanted to make sure that people didn't think I was pushing to never talk about anything—quite the opposite. You talk about the things that matter to your customers from the point of view of what you do for them.

Three Action Steps

1. When a crisis arises, set your opinion aside and ask questions to create a safe space for conversation that builds trust.

2. Remember what "lane" you're in when it comes to your business and what your customers need and expect from you.

3. Talk to your customers about things that matter to them from the perspective of what you do for them.

Connect with Bob Graham at www.linkedin.com/in/bob-graham/ or BreakthroughSolutions.co

PRODUCTIVITY & MINDSET

Focus on Physical Health | 227
with Melissa Wolak

Adjust Your Mindset | 232
with Andrew Mellen

Working with Your Life Partner | 236
with Amy Lindner-Lesser

Tap into Your Natural Intuition | 240
with Victoria Whitfield

Lessons from ADHD | 245
with Dr. Ari Tuckman

The Next Right Thing, for the Right Reasons,
with the Right Heart | 250
with Randy Pryor

Mindset Is an Inside Job | 255
with Blanca Vergara

PRODUCTIVITY & MINDSET

It is during our darkest moments that we must focus to see the light.

—Aristotle

While you may have considered yourself a productive person with a positive mindset in the past, the global pandemic challenged even the most efficient, effective business owners, uncovered gaps, strained relationships, and drained our collective energy. But it also allowed us to strip away the unnecessary and focus our efforts. These next interviews span from physical to mental to relational and spiritual well-being and how these things affect the work that we do.

Melissa Wolak of Melissa Hundley Wolak, LLC tells us how productivity is not just about what we do but is strongly correlated with the health of our brain. Melissa shares how to ensure our mindset starts with a healthy mind.

Andrew Mellen of Andrew Mellen, Inc delves into the topic of staying productive while working from home in the midst of a global pandemic. He answers the question of what is needed now that is different than in other times.

Amy Lindner-Lesser of the Rookwood Inn explores what is needed to be in business with your life partner. She explores boundaries, communication, office space, and ways to think outside the box.

Victoria Whitfield of Victoria Whitfield, LLC connects strategic meditation with systems for productivity that taps into your natural intuition and energy. She identifies the number one thing holding businesses back from growth and why organizations would do well to incorporate Eastern cultural practices into their business.

Dr. Ari Tuckman of PsyD specializes in Attention Deficit Hyperactivity Disorder (ADHD) in adults. Dr. Tuckman's unique expertise informs his approach to time management and productivity. In his interview, he shares lessons that can be applied from working with ADHD to our world of information overload, distraction, and uncertainty.

Randy Pryor of Hope for Separated Husbands brings a fresh perspective on the effects of your relationship on your mindset and productivity. He shares what to do to cut down on stress in your home and how to prioritize with the resources you have available.

Blanca Vergara of Your Looking Glass taps into the female lineage to identify a source of confidence, power, creativity, and abundance. Lessons to learn here are: your mindset is central to your success, how to tap fully into yourself, and ask for what you want.

Focus on Physical Health

Melissa Wolak
Transformation Coach, Speaker, Educator & Speech
Language Pathologist
Melissa Hundley Wolak, LLC

Melissa Wolak, MS, is a change-maker, speaker, and fierce advocate for creating more intention, resilience, and presence with conscious living despite stress and self-doubt or criticism. She coaches and speaks to motivated, intelligent professionals who are ready to create powerful mindset shifts, meaningful connections, and sustainable practices for self-expression, nourishment, and inner freedom. The foundation of her movement and unique system connects science and soul by incorporating her 23 years of experience, education with a bachelors and masters in communication science disorders, and her development of sustainable tools based in neuroscience, mindfulness, and practical function.

Main Takeaway

When you have a healthy mind and body, you can take risks and handle stress.

Questions

1. What role does mindset play in aligning and thriving in business and personal well-being?

2. How do we cultivate more focus and productivity and decrease feeling scattered in our work?

3. What is one mindset shift that can make an impact on a daily basis?

Interview: What do businesses need to know right now about mindset and sustainable change?

Mindset and sustainable change are critical. Looking at changes we can make that will stick. I love bringing the science together with the reality of what we're living in and helping people to understand the "why" of it working and that there is a reason behind it. It has been my experience that many people aren't thinking about the science behind mindset.

What role does mindset play in aligning and thriving in business and personal well-being?

When looking at mindset, the first thing we need is a healthy mind. A healthy mind requires nourishing, taking care of, food, and hydration. That's the foundation. That's where we will increase our bandwidth of what we can accomplish.

Many people aren't thinking "healthy mind," when they are thinking "mindset." They're not thinking, "How can I make my brain, my mind, and my body healthier?" They might be thinking about the thoughts but not necessarily connecting how important it is to have a healthy mind as the baseline for healthy thoughts.

Because of that, we have the physical and mental resilience to be able to take risks and make decisions when things are in a painful state of urgency, which we do in business. Having that foundation of getting back to basics and taking care of our mental and physical health is extremely important. I always like to mention that as part of the mindset. There's also the actual programming of our mind.

On the survival side, which almost everyone is tapping into at this point, when they're stressed, when there's chaos, when we're supposed to return something quickly, if you're on a deadline, it actually triggers our nervous system. Our nervous system gets a little flooded, and we start becoming reactionary. We don't want to be reacting constantly because then we're on the defensive, and we're putting out fires. Instead, we want to create this more intentional mindset that allows us to be resilient, respond, give ourselves a little bit of space so we can choose how we move forward.

How do we cultivate more focus and productivity and decrease feeling scattered in our work?

Focus on nutrition, hydration, sleep, exercise, and blood flow to cultivate mental, physical health. To tackle brain fog, take a five-minute walk. Seventy-five percent of America is dehydrated, which causes those individuals brain fog and headaches. Grab a glass of water, and save the cocktail for later on as a celebration because you were intentional, and you accomplished a lot.

As for the business part, first, set up the intention. What are your areas of impact? Instead of booking ourselves all day long with to-dos, think about, "How do I want to feel? What do I want to accomplish? And what matters most today?" Many of us are working from home.

For me, this morning, I had several things going on, but I picked three tasks intentionally, this interview being one of them. Then my daughter woke up, and she did not feel good. Today, we have wildfires going up in Colorado. And it seems like she has some smoke inhalation. I had set those intentions, so instead of thinking, "Oh, no, the day is ruined!" and allowing the negativity bias of, "How am I going to get all this done? There's just no way!"—I had cultivated a mindset of one inner calm with mindfulness practices. That was how I had decided to feel.

Second, before I got out of bed, I asked myself, "What are the three most important things I want to accomplish today?" Realistically, with some buffer time, just in case.

Buffer time is often what is missed. It is the space between appointments in case something goes wrong. Without it, you may feel like you are moving from thing to thing such that when that emergency comes up, there's no room for it.

What is one mindset shift that can make an impact on a daily basis?

I hear this all the time. "There's not enough time to do everything I want."

Almost everyone says that it comes from a scarcity mindset. That mindset can be detrimental in business. Sometimes we also put that towards our money in our charging. Shift that over to an abundance mindset such as, "I have the time to get what's important done."

Today, I had this interview. I am revamping my entire website. And I had one other thing that was very important. I paused to ask, "What is my intention?" Then I got up and I went for a walk. I made sure I had a great breakfast. I even did a dance class to get the energy moving. I've been taking care of my daughter. But having that priority list, I know what to keep coming back to. I'm not getting distracted by voicemail or email or other people's emergencies. I know what I am focusing on today. And I have that buffer time in there so that I can breathe. That's abundance and expansiveness.

Instead of cultivating a dialogue of, "I've got to do. I've got to do. I have to. I'm supposed to. I should," which is heavy and takes away from being able to create—we can act with intention.

We don't have to end the day feeling less than and judging and critical. I acknowledged that I completed what I needed to complete and nourished myself before the day went to hell in a handbasket. The food came my way. And I was able to be a good mom, take care of my daughter, and work from home. In doing so, we have learned to pivot.

When you have a healthy mind and body, you can take risks and handle stress.

Three Action Steps

1. Focus on your brain's physical health first: hydration, good food, exercise, and rest.

2. Start with intention. Decide what you want to feel and your three priority tasks for the day.

3. Shift to a belief that you do have all that you need to be successful—including time.

Connect with Melissa Wolak at
www.linkedin.com/in/melissahwolak/ or melissawolak.com or
opt-in bit.ly/RechargeandBreatheFreeGift for short audio
downloads that will allow you to do five-minute reset breaks so that
you can take charge.

Adjust Your Mindset

Andrew Mellen
Keynote Speaker, Executive Coach & Author
Andrew Mellen

Andrew Mellen is a keynote speaker, executive coach, and productivity and organizational expert. He's known as "The Most Organized Man in America" and is the author of the best-selling book *Unstuff Your Life!* and *The Most Organized Man in America's Guide to Moving.*

Main Takeaway

Adjusting your mindset to adapt to unpredictability is key. When your mindset is correct, you will be better able to handle obstacles and challenges.

Questions

1. What do we need to know about moving our work from the workplace to home or even back into the workplace after being home?

2. What are the things that business owners need to know or focus on that they can control?

3. Is there a blind spot that businesses are experiencing right now?

Interview: What do businesses need to know right now about productivity?

Productivity during a pandemic is definitely a unique challenge. With companies being thrust into new ways of doing business, it's only natural that there are challenges to productivity and business itself. Andrew Mellen is a keynote speaker, executive coach, and productivity and organizational expert who is tackling what businesses need to know right now about productivity.

What do we need to know about moving our work from the workplace to home or even back into the workplace after being home?

You need to adjust your mindset to adapting—adapting to the fact that nothing is going to be predictable.

One of the biggest stumbling blocks that people are struggling with is the idea that this is a temporary situation and that things are going to reset themselves back to normal. And when things don't go back to "normal," people get thrown for an emotional, psychological, and even physical loop. The sooner you can let go of this need for things to reset and walk forward with a certain amount of grace and appreciation for the unpredictable, the easier it will be for you to adapt to the next thing that happens.

Whatever the challenge you are facing might be, if you can approach it with a sense of, "This is not surprising . . ." the better off you will be. For example, you may find the micro facts are surprising, but the overarching fact that "something has changed" and you couldn't predict it is no longer surprising—that will help you immensely.

Suzy Kassem, an American writer and poet, said, "Life is no different than the weather. Not only is it unpredictable, but it shows us a new perspective of the world every day." And while many people thrive on predictability, are you ready to change your expectation that things are going to be unpredictable for a while?

What are the things that business owners need to know or focus on that they can control?

My suggestion is to control the things you can control. Here are some examples of things you can control:

- What time you show up for work
- How you work
- How you stay focused

These are things you have complete control of. Turn the attention back on yourself and your environment to help you face the more unpredictable portions of your life.

And then, once you've helped yourself, it's time to look at your business. Start with some of the big things.

- If you are going to be working remotely, do you still need an office?
- If you still have an office, are you going back to the office?
- What does the office need to look like?
- If most of your people are going to be telecommuting, how do you support that transition?
- What long-term protocols and standard operating procedures need to be established for doing business?
- How are we going to share digital assets?

Answering these questions and having everyone aware and on the same page means that there will be less friction when the things we can't control crop up.

Businesses that have really good systems in place are easily adapting to the changes. Businesses that are lacking in good systems and communication are struggling during this time. If you find that your business is struggling, now may be the time to get your systems and processes in place to not only help you now but moving forward also.

Is there a blind spot that businesses are experiencing right now?

It goes back to mindset again and seeing this as an opportunity. Not an opportunity to exploit COVID-19 financially, but as an opportunity to take inventory of your business. Use this time as a chance to improve the things you want or need to improve. Don't procrastinate. Make a choice to meet your obstacles head-on.

When was the last time you took a hard look at your business? Taking inventory of your business is the first step to improving it— and it can be done during difficult times.

Three Action Steps

1. Adjust your mindset to the fact that nothing is going to be predictable and that you are going to need to adapt to change.

2. Focus on the things you can control—both for yourself and for your business.

3. Use this time as an opportunity to improve your business by taking a hard look at what you are doing.

Connect with Andrew Mellen at
www.linkedin.com/in/andrewmellen/ and AndrewMellen.com

Working with
Your Life Partner

Amy Lindner-Lesser
Proprietor, Founder
The Rookwood Inn

Amy Lindner Lesser is the proprietor of the Rookwood Inn. She began that role in 1996 with her husband. She also wears many other hats such as social worker, Justice of the Peace minister, and life coach.

Main Takeaway

Working with those you love and live with requires clarity in roles, space, schedules, and breaks.

Questions

1. What would you say to the business owners who are running a business together, living together, loving together, raising a family together, and suddenly, there's no space in the house and there's no space in the office?

2. Is there some missing piece? Something that businesses can be doing that they're not right now that might help their situation?

Interview: What do businesses need to know right now about working with your life partner?

If you are in business with someone you live with, Amy Lindner-Lesser, proprietor of the Rookwood Inn, Justice of the Peace, and the Co-Founder's Coach, shares how to work with those you love.

I'm somebody who's gone through all kinds of life transitions. I'm a parent of two adult children, a grandma with one more on the way, and a widow. I was a caregiver for my mother and step-father for the last five years of their lives. I've had lots of business experience and personal experience. I've run the Inn now for almost twenty-one years on my own. My husband passed away two and a half years after buying me in, which was something I never expected to be facing—being single, single parenting, or owning a business and operating it on my own.

You have hit just about every life transition and life experience that one could have, and yet you are still so upbeat and still so ready to share and help others. Recently, you've turned that energy and attention to a new adventure, I would say, but certainly not new to you—and that is, as the Co-Founders Coach. In this program, you are helping couples who are in business together. This is so relevant right now, with so many folks at home, they're operating their business, there used to be some time when they could escape from all of this joint venturing that they're doing. But now there's no space.

What would you say to the business owners who are running a business together, living together, loving together, raising a family together, and suddenly, there's no space in the house and there's no space in the office?

With all of us being stuck at home, or privileged to be at home, people who never work together, are now working together because they're sharing space. What I found in our first two years of owning the Inn, where we lived here and worked together, was that it was really important to have very clearly defined roles. Each of us found what our strengths were, what we would agree to do, and what we would let the other person do. This ensured that we didn't have arguments about whose responsibility it was.

Co-founders are intentionally in business together. But now that we're all home, we're de facto in business together. My husband is working upstairs, and he has a paid nine-to-five job, and I'm running my business downstairs. The kids are doing school just outside of my office door. We're all in this situation. Clearly defining those roles is essential.

Ensure clearly delineated spaces so that you're not pushing each other out of the way.

Make sure you're not in a corner in the dining room or the kitchen, where everybody is walking through. For those of us used to having an office to go to where we don't have the interruptions of our children or our spouse—it's a new game.

Find ways to separate. Whether it's when things get sort of heated, or a decision needs to be made, or somebody's emotions get out of hand, it's important to be able to separate physically. You could leave the room, work in a different space, or go out and take a walk. Or it could be running errands. Shopping is one of my least favorite things. But doing it was a way for me to get out and get away from business and have to think about something else.

You don't have to do your business all the time. You can have your own space. You can meet with your customers separately. Having clearly defined spaces, breaks, and time is an extension of clearly defined roles.

Is there some missing piece? Something that businesses can be doing that they're not right now that might help their situation.

For some businesses, it's not terribly hard to pivot. There may be ways to take things online. But for many of us, I know I struggled for the first few weeks, asking, "How do I take an 'Inn experience' where people come to get away from the stress and relax and change it into something different?" I could take it anywhere else. So, I developed packages to bring our experience home with you. And those are available online. I think it is so important to find other businesses, either in the same field that you're in, or maybe even in a completely different field, and collaborate

For me, it is an interview series that I'll be starting. I'm doing interviews with a lot of the cultural venues, the museums, the theater groups, and the like here. I ask them to tell us where their facility or venue is and give us a secret, something nobody else might know. I am using this as a way to remind our guests that there are still things here when it's time for them to be able to travel, and it keeps all of us in the forefront. We've talked about selling each other's products on online stores or when we reopen to be able to sell and gift shops. I have been working with more coaches and talking about collaborating by offering retreats here at Inn. We can make plans for when the environment opens up again.

This is a fantastic time for relationship building.

Three Action Steps

1. Create clearly defined roles, spaces, schedules, and breaks.

2. Collaborate with other businesses.

3. Build relationships.

Connect with Amy Lindner-Lesser on www.linkedin.com/in/AmyL1/

Tap into Your Natural Intuition

Victoria Whitfield
Business Reiki Master
Victoria Whitfield, LLC

As the world's first Business Reiki Master and hostess of the five-star rated *Journeypreneur Podcast* on iTunes, Sensei Victoria Whitfield helps empathic entrepreneurs and leaders stay grounded and clear as they navigate the emotional roller-coaster of business development by using the power of strategic meditation. She is a published author, a successful six-figure energy healer, and she has toured the world showing heart-centered and growth-minded leaders how to get connected to their natural intuition and truly be visionary, so they can work less and increase their impact. Call her when you or another entrepreneur you love needs to detox from toxic coaching overload and bust through money blocks and abundance plateaus in life and business.

Main Takeaway

Understanding your energy and that of your business, and using methodologies like strategic meditation, can be the missing link between the systems and strategies you have and the growth you desire.

Questions

1. What is the number one thing holding businesses back from the growth that they desire?

2. What is "woo-woo" and how does it apply in the corporate world?

3. What methodology allows a business to tap into their energy and natural intuition?

Interview: What do businesses need to know right now about money blocks?

Sensei Victoria Whitfield has toured the world, showing heart-centered and growth-minded leaders how to get connected to their natural intuition and truly be visionary so they can work less and increase their impact, which as visionary healers, is so important. The big question is, "How does this apply to me? What do I need strategic meditation for in the corporate world?"

What is the number one thing holding businesses back from the growth that they desire?

The one thing that we need the most right now as leaders, to really take our vision and business to the next level is energy awareness. We can get stagnant and begin to plateau at levels of growth and development, forward momentum plateaus and slows the movement of the business. You can be doing all the right things, doing what the consultants do, following the protocols that you've set up before, working as best you could, but the plateau keeps coming. There's a certain point where it becomes more of an energetic issue, rather than just a systems issue.

What do I mean by energy? Answering this question is especially important—defining the word "energy" for leaders who may not be familiar with "woo-woo" talk.

What is the definition of "woo-woo," and how does it apply in the corporate world?

This is softer skills management. It has to do with emotional intelligence: not just IQ, but we're talking about EQ as well—measuring the level of relatability in leadership, morale in organizations as well as employee wellness. When you're looking at improving your corporation's wellness and human resources programs, the types of programs that can take things to the right next level are often a little bit out of the box. They could come from different and divergent cultures, such as Eastern medicine and philosophies. But these programs are better suited to help maintain your team's health and well-being outside of just a medical context. It is not just about keeping you and your employees off the operating table, but instead it's about how you can live life feeling well, working well, and getting better and better over time.

To a Western mindset, it can be classified as "woo-woo," other cultural practices for health and well-being. But I just want to take that "woo-woo" word and smash it on the floor, like the brittle glass box that it is, and let it go.

This stuff is extremely relevant to the business environment. The research you've done and the work you've done with your clients has enabled you to help them break free from a lot of the fears, the "blockages" that have held them back through the strategic meditation and other methodologies that you use.

What methodology allows a business to tap into their energy and natural intuition?

Strategic meditation is meditation done with purpose, within a professional context. The reason why we do that is to manage the force behind action, the force behind focus, and that force is energy. Yes, you may know exactly what needs to get done. But if you're feeling drained and exhausted, not just on a physical level of exhaustion, but also emotionally exhausted, unable to move past this obstacle here or there, then that can end up being an energetic issue. Being able to bring meditation in during strategic points in the growth and momentum of a given organization can help open up what may be a roadblock and turn it into a spring-board for new growth.

Many businesses are looking at the way they've done things in the past and what's happening now and thinking, "I'm worried about the world, I'm worried about my business, I'm worried about my clients, I'm worried about my employees." Energetically, if we're speaking that way, there's this disconnect. What should a business do?

A business can absolutely manifest a momentum or money block for sure through this type of thinking.

"I'm worried. I'm worried. I'm worried" places your focus—and your force behind your action—on to generating more worry, rather than generating solutions.

This is okay. It's normal and natural; we're not trying to completely discount "worry" itself. However, it can drain your creative and productive energy. It's at this very point that you can bring in meditation, strategically. In the work that I do, we set up structures to make sure that you're bringing in meditation at the times that we've seen tend to create the most energetic blockage in organizations. You can tell that the energy of that organization is either low or stagnant because the sales are stagnating. The opt-ins or the conversions are stagnating. In turn, if you meditate in a certain way, you can restore or even reset your energy, and then go to the issue having your thumb on the pulse of your people—feeling that connection to, "Yes, we're clicked in. We understand each other. We're flowing, we're progressing."

But if there's a disconnect, in a way that you can't exactly explain—such as, when the numbers should be working, given all of what is being done—then it could be more of an ener-getic block, and the money will reflect that. This in fact is why I'm so grateful to work with entrepreneurs and business owners, because we can look at the money and see how it is responding to their energetic work.

Using strategic meditation to tap into your natural intuition, tap into deeper knowing and understanding, and then using that to do the strategic planning is a magic formula.

Three Action Steps

1. Become energy aware. Notice what you are putting out into the world and what you are attracting back to you.

2. Be open to new ways of solving the problems in your business.

3. Learn strategic meditation to apply it to your business.

Connect with Sensei Victoria Whitfield at linkedin.com/in/senseivictoriawhitfield/ or VictoriaWhitfield.com Contact for a one-to-one conversation to discern the problem in your organization or in your business's growth and how to integrate strategic meditation to ensure the problem is converted into your springboard.

Lessons from ADHD

Dr. Ari Tuckman
Psychologist, Author & Speaker
Ari Tuckman, PsyD

Dr. Ari Tuckman, PsyD, MBA, is a psychologist, author, and speaker specializing in ADHD, which informs his approach to time management and productivity for all clients.

Main Takeaway

People with ADHD have difficulty managing multiple goals and priorities, but when they clarify their goals, it helps to make choices easier for them.

Questions

1. What lessons does ADHD offer everyone when it comes to productivity?
2. Why is it so hard to do the right thing in the moment?
3. How do we handle uncertainty?

Interview: What do businesses need to know right now about time management and productivity?

Dr. Ari Tuckman is a psychologist, author, and speaker specializing in ADHD, which informs his approach to time management and productivity for all clients. For business owners, his approach to interacting with employees and clients is extremely relevant, and he's sharing what businesses need to know right now about time management and productivity—especially if you have ADHD or employees with ADHD.

What lessons does ADHD offer everyone when it comes to productivity?

The challenge for all of us as we go through this information overload world that we live in is to sort through all the information and to make choices. You need to make choices about what is the most important, about what to do first. What do I do second? What do I perhaps never do?

We're balancing multiple goals and multiple priorities. Some things are really fun, and we want to do them. Some things are really painfully boring or cognitively challenging, and we're not so sure we want to do them, but we probably should.

This is the world that we live in, and moment by moment, we're making choices about where to put our attention, and where to put our energy or cognitive energy.

For folks with ADHD, really, what separates ADHD from folks without ADHD is that ADHD is kind of an exacerbation. It's like on a spectrum, so to speak, with this kind of general human tendency that we all tend to favor the present over the future. So, in other words, what's going to be more interesting, what's going to be more important right now, as opposed to what's going to be more interesting or what's going to be more beneficial for me later.

For example, this is why people suck at saving for retirement because going out to dinner, or in this world ordering in dinner tonight, is way more interesting than putting money away into retirement that I may not need for 30 years—even though it's going to be twice as much or five times as much as what we spent on dinner tonight. ADHD is that—but more so. People with ADHD have more difficulty letting go of the distractions, the temptations of the moment, and instead of acting towards the thing that's better for the future. So, as a result, they tend to procrastinate more. And while procrastinating is something we all do, folks with ADHD tend to do it even more so.

Balancing multiple goals and priorities can be challenging for anyone, but ADHD makes it even more challenging. People with ADHD have to decide where to put their attention and energy—and while prioritizing may be a simple skill for you—it's more difficult for them. Being cognizant of the process that people with ADHD work through can help you better understand the choices that they are making.

Why is it so hard to do the right thing in the moment?

The reason is, in order to think towards the future, we have to disengage from the present. So, if you get absorbed in something really interesting right now, you're not pausing to think about, "Well, is this really the best thing I should be doing? Is this the best use of my time? What is coming down the pike that I should probably start thinking about and acting on sooner rather than later on?"

A big part of managing ADHD is about managing the environment. While medication is very effective for ADHD, if you can't change the distractibility inside your own mind, then the thing you do is change the world around you. So, often you'll limit how much comes at you. You will purposely set certain things aside in order to have a plan or to have clear goals and priorities. Because if you don't really know your priorities, how do you decide what is the best thing to do in this moment versus in the next moment versus next week? Having a clear sense of what your big goals and priorities are is important, and then the individual choices flow down from that.

Doing the right thing in the moment to move your business forward is important. Goals and priorities are essential for making that happen—as are limiting the distractions. These are lessons we can all use.

How do we handle uncertainty?

Uncertainty is always a part of life. It was a thing in December before any of us heard of COVID. We've always been dealing with uncertainty.

I think what's changed is that all of a sudden, we got hit with a big wad of uncertainty—all at once. For example, those of us who all of a sudden had to transition working from home, there were lots of questions to work through, such as:

- How do we do this again?
- How do I do those old things?
- What are these new things I've got to do?
- How do I get my kid figured out on Zoom?

A lot changed really quickly. But life has transitions, and things change. So, it's not different in kind; it's just different in scale.

The quarantine situation has had numerous effects. For some people, it's really been helpful to wind down a bit and really focus on what's most important. It's also made simple things more complicated.

Sometimes transitions like this can be an opportunity to think about what is truly the most important to you. While there's more uncertainty ahead yet, it's important to have some sense of this is what I'm trying to do. Here's what's most important, and here's what I can let go of. Doing this makes it a bit easier to navigate some of the uncertainty, and that makes it easier to act rather than to not act.

Unfortunately, doing something doesn't mean you're doing the right thing. Sometimes we need to just wait for things to evolve and unfold in order to know what the best thing to do is.

People with ADHD tend to be more impulsive, meaning they're not as good at waiting. They're more likely to leap before they look, and it's one of those things that you can cut both ways.

There are definitely a lot of entrepreneurs who have ADHD. And the benefit is if you're one of the first to leap, you may wind up in an empty space and be able to really establish yourself and make that space your own. The problem is if you leap without looking, you may wind up jumping off a cliff and realize why nobody else has jumped into that space.

There's a delicate balance. If you're too cautious, you miss opportunities, but if you rush in too quickly, you can get crushed early on. Different people have different tolerances for how much risk they're willing to take. You need to know for yourself what's the right amount.

Uncertainty has always existed is a powerful truth. But dealing with large amounts of uncertainty is the game-changer right now. And deciding how you're going to react to it will make the biggest difference.

Three Action Steps

1. Clarify your goals and priorities.

2. Clear goals and priorities will allow you to make choices that are good for your business now and in the future.

3. Know that uncertainty has always existed, but use the current uncertainty to decide what is important to you and what is not.

Connect with Ari Tuckman at Ari@TuckmanPsych.com

The Next Right Thing, for the Right Reasons, with the Right Heart

Randy Pryor
Owner & Coach
Hope for Separated Husbands

For the past 10 years, Randy Pryor has been working with CEOs, executives, and other professionals who are struggling in their marriages. Randy has been specializing in reconnecting separated husbands with their wives because there aren't as many resources available—specifically for men—as there are for women. As we all know, if your home life is in turmoil, it's difficult to focus on your work, and both your marriage and your business suffer.

Main Takeaway

Work on yourself and ask yourself, "How can I support my partner today?"

Questions

1. What can business people do right now to improve their home life so they can become more productive at work—especially if they're working remotely?

2. What do businessmen and businesswomen need to know right now about repairing struggling relationships?

3. Why are there so many more resources available for women than for men?

Interview: What do businesses need to know right now about relationships?

There are not a lot of conversations going on that talk about relationships as they relate to your business, yet it's a really important conversation to have. Randy works with CEOs, executives, and other professionals who are struggling in their marriages. Randy has been specializing in reconnecting separated husbands with their wives because there aren't as many resources available specifically for men as there are for women. And, as we all know, if your home life is in turmoil, it's difficult to focus on your work, and both your marriage and your business suffer. It's good to remember that you're a whole person, not just a person at home or a person at work, and Randy is sharing what businesses need to know right now about relationships.

What can business people do right now to improve their home life so they can become more productive at work—especially if they're working remotely?

That's a really great question. Apparently, in China, due to the COVID-19 lockdown, the divorce rate just went up 25 percent. So, people were stuck at home, and then a lot of people just went right to their lawyers and said, "I'm out."

Basically, they're saying, "We need to change the situation."

It's just not working because they're used to one thing, like being at work eight hours, and doing the normal life, and now obviously, this whole thing has been changed. It's really tough.

Fortunately, there are some things that you can do.

First of all, we should realize that the other person is living a life that is just as upside down as ours. It's completely different, but their life is as different as ours is. I know that we say,

"Well, just cut each other some slack." That's obviously true. But it's more than that. There's much more than just giving each other more grace. Yes, we absolutely do that. But I think one of the most important things to do is if there's a lot of stress in the home, and that's usually what we're talking about, is to cut down some stress and be less stressed yourself. Do this instead of expecting somebody else to be less stressed.

How do we do that? One of my favorite things to do is a gratitude five. I know you've heard this before. Spend five minutes every morning, being and feeling grateful for what you already have.

It's not about just listing 10 things. It's not, "Here are the 10 things I'm grateful for." That's a good start. That's really great. But what I'm saying is take five minutes to actually feel your gratitude. It doesn't matter what it's about. Let's say I'm grateful for my dog. I love my puppy, and I'm very grateful for my dog. Great! But don't just check that off your list. Actually feel the gratitude. Ask yourself, why are you grateful? Think about that for a minute. Just spend five minutes at the beginning of your day—right in the morning before you jump into work, before all this stuff is going on. You know the phrase "Count your blessings." But don't just count them, don't just check them off—actually feel the gratitude. It'll destress everything. It'll be a great way to start the day, and you can have a quick little gratitude break anytime you want throughout the day, and it's the most effective thing that I've found for reducing stress on everybody's part.

This reminds me of Geoffrey Blake. Geoffrey has started a global gratitude movement called, "Global Gratitude Jar." And it's actually how I start my day. I spend a moment to say what I'm grateful for. And it really does change the dynamic, change how you feel, and perhaps gives you a new way to look at what we're all experiencing in this particular moment.

What do businessmen and businesswomen need to know right now about repairing struggling relationships?

If you're in a relationship, one of the best things you can do for your partner is what I call "putting them first." So, thinking about them, and I would say the operative word is proactively. You don't just want to say to your partner, "Let me know what you need, and I'll provide it for you." You want to ask yourself, "How could I make their life a little bit easier today?" Do it in that same little five-minute time or add another five minutes. If they're stressed out, ask yourself, how can I relieve some pressure? If they're dealing with (whatever they're going through), how could I help them? Maybe it's a simple little bouquet of flowers on the table. Maybe it's a text, a simple text message that lets them know that you appreciate them, and that you're thinking about them. And it doesn't have to be big. You don't have to run out and buy them a new iPhone. That's not the idea. The idea is to let them know that you're on their side, you're there for support, and again, it's—proactive. It's not just waiting until they need you. It's actively asking yourself, "How can I make their day a little bit better today?" Then, go do it.

The point is, you only have control of one thing, and that's you. You don't have any control over anybody else, or what they're feeling or doing, or what they "should" or "shouldn't" be doing. That's an illusion—to have control over someone else. You don't have it. All you can control is yourself. So, set out to do the next right thing. My motto is this: Just do the next right thing, for the right reasons, with the right heart, and leave the outcome to God. Because if you're doing the next right thing, you don't need to worry about the outcome. Because you don't have control over what somebody else is going to do or think or feel about it anyway.

We talk about this in business a lot—taking control of the things you can control. So, it makes sense that it works for relationships, too. By taking care of yourself, and proactively looking at helping your partner, you are doing what you can at the moment for your relationship.

Why are there so many more resources available for women than for men?

The bottom-line answer is that it's because women are made differently than men. No big revelation there. God gave women the nurturing, the intuition, and the emotions, etc. So, they have no problem going out and picking up the resources and reaching out for help.

But God made us men different. We're logical. And we've been given the need to fix things. That's what we do. That's our entire life. If something's broken, let's fix it. And that's where we focus. So unfortunately, along the way, we've been raised that to need help in the relationship area is some kind of weakness. It makes us feel like we're weak. If we can't figure it out ourselves, like they say, "Pull yourself up by your own bootstraps," somehow we're weak. Or "Men shouldn't cry." That's how we're raised. And while I understand this, what it also means is that men don't reach out for help in the relationship area. They will for other kinds of coaching, but they don't in the relationship area.

So, if you've got women who will buy the resources, DVDs, books, etc., the authors are going to make them for women because they're going to sell, and that's why there are very few resources for men.

Three Action Steps

1. Take responsibility and reduce your own stress which will cut down on the stress you may be experiencing at home.

2. Spend five minutes every day being—and feeling—grateful for what you have.

3. Do the next right thing, for the right reasons, with the right heart, and leave the outcome to God.

Connect with Randy Pryor
at www.linkedin.com/in/coachrandypryor/
or at his website: hope4sh.com

Mindset Is an Inside Job

Blanca Vergara
Soul & Business Mentor
Your Looking Glass

Blanca Vergara is a soul and business mentor for international female business owners. She helps them transmute their female lineage into an unlimited source of power and abundance. After working with her, they succeed and bloom on every level.

Main Takeaway

Money mindset is an inside job. When we tap into who we are with confidence, we tap into knowledge and creativity that allows us to be successful, shake off outdated beliefs, and ask for what we want.

Questions

1. What are the "wealth destroyers" that are hurting each and every woman's business?

2. How does your background enable you to be so successful at this?

3. Is there something about this time that is important, especially for women?

Interview: What do businesses need to know right now about money mindset for women entrepreneurs?

Wealth destroyers, what are they? And how are they hurting women's businesses?

Whatever statistics you look at, women are performing worse than men. When we grow old, we are number one in poverty. Just 6% of the Fortune 500 companies have female CEOs, 2% of VC funds are granted to companies founded by women. We could blame it on the system or we can blame it on men, but blame doesn't help us.

The big thing is what happens between our ears. When we take responsibility, we become aware of what is happening between our ears. Why do I have this nagging voice telling me to shut up? Do not show up or not reply to email? Don't go to the conference? Don't raise my price? Don't make that offer?

It is not you. It is really ancestral. We're talking about mental programming that comes from 1000s of years ago. At the end of the 19th century, in England, still women were sold—I'm not talking about a millennium ago.[3]

To change that mindset is the key that we need.

What is destroying our wealth? What is between our ears? It is our subconscious beliefs, the things that stop us, the inner saboteurs. This guilt for making money. This shame for having wealth. This codependent behavior. You know we want to save everybody. Those sorts of things keep us small.

And this is true for women at every financial level. It works for those women who give their coaching for free. It's also applicable to the women who already have a big business of several million, yet they don't delegate or build systems that would replace them. They need control.

There is a new devil at every level. But it is the very same

---

3 — People continue to be sold into slavery. It is estimated at 40.3 million people continue to live in slavery according to the UN's International Labour Organization and the Walk Free Foundation. Women make up 71% of that number.

thing. Like an onion, we have to peel it, and we get stronger and peel it and get stronger.

We're talking about strength in a feminine way: more compassionate, more centered, more inclusive. Our strength doesn't mean to substitute men or emulate them.

It's not that we become more masculine. That's where we create the power that you're talking about the confidence and the belief system. It's by becoming more feminine that we create that energy and that creativity and the ideas that are going to destroy the wealth destroyers.

Where does this understanding for you come from? How did you start to look into this ancestral history of women not showing up as themselves and having these beliefs?

I have recently recalled a repressed teenage memory. When I was 14 years old, I was sexually abused. During the healing of this gigantic trauma, I realized that self-worth is intricately linked with sexuality. This link has ancestrally affected our ability to talk about money because it feels dirty; we feel dirty. We feel shameful.

I've discovered that I was not alone in this. It is just like fractals. It's everywhere. You look at the story of Eve, you see the story of the witches, you see the story of Mary Magdalene, you see the story of Margaret Thatcher or Madonna—and these are just a copy of a copy of a copy of a copy. So, of course, it comes from a personal story, me, Blanca, but it comes from my aunt, and my mother, and my grandma.

When I began to look, I thought, "Holy cow! It is not just me, Blanca. It is all the women on the planet. It started as a personal story. I began as a very masculine woman—an "A" type. I went to university. I got my MBA. I worked as a big executive. I had a flashy car paid for by the company, earning loads of money, deciding over millions of euros in an English company.

There was something in my mind that said I could not have love and money at the same time. I believed that I could not be wealthy and happy and healthy all that the same time. I believed I could not make a lot of money without giving things up. This belief is the thing that I've been helping women to change. You can have it the way you want it.

Is there something about this time that is important, especially for women?

That's so powerful. Right now, there is a lot of uncertainty in the world. People are asking questions. They're making new decisions about what direction they want to go in in their life. They're deciding how to use their time and their money and their energy differently.

I believe that we are in a great awakening. A consciousness awakening. We are opening. It looks like a divine force has come to wake us up. With worldwide lockdown, we've been forced to open our journals, to open our hearts to meditating, to whatever religion people express—even if they don't believe in a God. We are coming back to what is important. What is my mission in life? What are my values? What is important for me? People are making decisions about quitting that job, career, or marriage. They are noticing it is not what you love, but what you tolerate. When you stop tolerating—what doesn't give you life? Or, as Marie Kondo said, "What doesn't give you joy?" Then you elevate. You ask, "What do I want? What brings me joy? What brings me into what Gay Hendricks called my 'zone of genius'?"

How can I welcome more wealth, more happiness, more harmony? And do that consistently? Do that daily. It's a daily practice. With every breath you take, you can choose a better job, relationship, or payment. Doing so attracts money.

We have come full circle: As we become aware of what we have been tolerating and focus instead on what we want truly want, more of the latter will show up in our reality.

This is the thing that changes wealth destruction, so that it attracts money, it attracts abundance, health, joy, balance, ecology, and good relationships.

We need only stop tolerating and pay attention to what we want and be willing to make a statement as such.

Three Action Steps

1. Start with your own mindset. Understand that you have responsibility for how you feel and your outcomes.

2. Allow yourself to be fully you—a balance of the best of the masculine and the feminine.

3. Tolerate less and focus on what you really want.

Connect with Blanca Vergara at
www.linkedin.com/in/blancavergara/ or www.blancavergara.com/

TECHNOLOGY

Cybersecurity | 264
with Ryan Barrett

TECHNOLOGY

Any sufficiently advanced technology is equivalent to magic.
—Sir Arthur C. Clarke

Our final section focuses on technology. Surprisingly this was not a bigger focus in the interviews, but it was a critical piece of conversation as workforces moved to work from home. Ben Chai, from the section on Strategy, identified the challenge that has opened up in creating security off-site. Schools globally moved to online instruction. There was a need to increase connectivity for work, school, and healthcare. Bandwidth was tested as work and play collided, and we collectively binge-watched our way through the early days of quarantine.

Ryan Barrett of Oram Corporate Advisors joins us to talk specifically about cybersecurity and what is needed to protect our data and transactions, what we need to be watching out for, and what we do when we are hacked.

Cybersecurity

Ryan Barrett
Network Security Designer & Information Architect
Oram Corporate Advisors

Ryan Barrett seeks to enhance small and medium-sized businesses and broaden their knowledge of information security. He has strong interpersonal skills, the ability to adapt and learn quickly, a vast understanding of complex business procedures, corporate infrastructure, and the fortitude to handle the unexpected.

Main Takeaway

Creating multiple layers of security is the best way to protect your company and your data from a cybersecurity attack.

Questions

1. What do business owners need to know about cyber-security threats?

2. What should we be looking at for ourselves or our employees beyond the first level of protection for data?

3. What should we be monitoring for? Is there something beyond our data that we should be looking at for security purposes?

Interview: What do businesses need to know right now about cybersecurity?

Ryan Barrett has spent the majority of his career consulting with organizations where data is critical to their business. He's seen technologies evolve into one of the most critical components to ensure a viable and scalable operation. With the current climate, and with so many businesses that have transitioned their employees to work from home and are transitioning them back, there's a lot to think about when it comes to keeping your company data secure. Ryan is sharing what businesses need to know right now about cybersecurity.

What do business owners need to know about cybersecurity threats?

The biggest thing that businesses need to know is that your information that you think is private—it really isn't.

There are many different instances out there—for example, with passwords for your everyday activities, your email, Facebook, LinkedIn, whatever—that have most likely have been compromised in the past.

You don't realize that the nefarious actors out there already know that password, and so, multifactor authentication is the absolute way it has to be.

What does that mean? Here's something that we've all done. You log into your bank account, and they send you a text message to make sure it's really you signed into the bank account. What that allows for is that if your password does get compromised out there on the dark web, and nefarious actors then try to use that password, you're always going to get that second-factor text message that asks you to please enter this code that we've sent you.

I would say that as a business owner, you have to realize that your passwords may have already been compromised from many different services, not because they're trying to hack your computer. But LinkedIn has been compromised. Staples has been compromised. Facebook has been compromised. So, change your password often. Always use multi-factor authentication and keep your information as secure as possible.

LastPass is our favorite password reader/manager.

And what's so great about LastPass? What's so great is that I don't know any of my passwords. Why is that? Why can someone say that they don't know their passwords? With something like LastPass, I know one password to unlock my LastPass or to unlock my password generator. And that allows me to create a Facebook password that I don't know—it creates a 16-digit password of all different characters and numbers, and it auto-fills it on my iPhone. It auto-fills in on my web browser, and I don't need to know it. And therefore, even if it does get asked or guessed in some weird fashion, it doesn't matter; I can change it in an instant.

LastPass can auto-generate a password for you really quick.

We can take simple steps to help protect our data. And the first step is really being mindful about our passwords. It's about being mindful about changing them and using things like a password generator to make sure that we're secure.

What should we be looking at for ourselves or our employees beyond the first level of protection for data?

We've discussed a password manager and multifactor authentication. Next, I would say dark web monitoring.

My email address is one piece of this password. So, whatever your email may be, I would monitor the dark web to see what they know about me. So, if I use the password "yellow," or "Google" or "green," or whatever it may be, and I do some variations of that, I have to be mindful that if I use that password, people already know that—so that's one key thing.

We always use our email addresses as the first token, and the second is the password, so anything that you can do to augment that would be ideal for a business owner today.

Are you monitoring your information on the dark web? Do you know how to do this? It may be time to reach out to an expert who can assist you with these things in order to protect your data and your business.

What should we be monitoring for? Is there something beyond our data that we should be looking at for security purposes?

It's not about if you will get hacked; it's when you will get hacked.

What we need to envision are layers of security. So, your network, your firewall, and your router should all be updated to the latest firmware or revisions. Your computer should have antivirus and anti-malware software. You should be using multifactor authentication for all the apps that you use on the web.

All of these little layers allow for a penetration to happen to your network or computer, but what you hope will eventually happen is that one of these layers will catch it before it gets to you and your family and your business. And that's what we always want to layer it up. It's like a bulletproof vest. There are multiple layers of that vest that help prevent a bullet from hitting the target.

What layers do you have in place to protect your data? And when was the last time you had them updated or reviewed to make sure you are doing all you can to keep your company safe from hackers?

Three Action Steps

1. Protect your passwords with a password manager, such as LastPass, and multifactor authentication.

2. Monitor the dark web to see what is known about you and your business.

3. Create multiple layers of security to protect your business and your data from an inevitable hack.

Connect with Ryan Barrett at
www.linkedin.com/in/ryanoramsaybarrett/

Conclusion

We learned from these interviews that adaptation is the catalyst to rebuild the world. Perhaps we knew it all along, but it took a pandemic that forced shutdowns and imposed severe impediments to our normal lives to force the lesson into our minds. Now we must dig into the lessons within this book and apply them. Let me leave you with something I have learned from conversing with the 45 experts in this book; you don't have to do it all, go deep with just one. Find your favorite, do the recommended steps, reach out to the expert and make the changes that you now know will make a difference in your business.

Here are the highlights:

Strategy

We learned that we need to always look for the opportunities that exist around us at all times. Do not be so tied to the original plan that you are unwilling to change but be sure you are always checking back in with that plan and ready to shift when the conditions require it.

Sales

The formula for reaching prospects and closing sales requires that you always connect, always converse, always make an offer, and do it all from an authentic desire to serve others.

Leadership

Leadership requires clarity, confidence, and compassion. You can learn these skills first to become a better leader and then share the techniques with your people. Bring your full self to your work as well as a positive mindset that will expand to touch all those in your organization.

Financial

The ins and outs of finance change constantly, so keep a close eye on your numbers and look to expert advisors to keep abreast of the most current information and guidance. Build reserves, continue to spend, but make sure to review your insurance options, health care, and tax strategies.

Communication

Authentic communication to your audience through storytelling is the way to connect emotionally to your audience. Build trust with clear, consistent engagement that shares your expertise in a way that connects with the real problems your ideal prospects are experiencing. Body language and words matter to create an experience that connects.

Connection & Collaboration

In the section on Sales, connection was emphasized as the main way to continue to drive business. In this section, the focus was on how to connect. Choose one or two strategies to take action on: collaborative partnerships, virtual networking, LinkedIn, video, or building your own network

People

The shift to work from home changed the scene dramatically on how we recruit, hire, and interact with our employees, contractors, and team. Don't stop recruiting, some of your best talent may have just become available and may now have fewer geographic bounds. Invest in your people and show them you value them by communicating clear expectations. Our employees' mental health cannot be ignored, especially in times of global stress.

Diversity, Inclusion, Equity & Belongingness

No longer can paying attention to diversity in your workplace be a "nice to have" or an afterthought. A focus on diversity and inclusion raises the bar for all employees and will help your business grow. Fostering a culture of belonging means being willing to have conversations, to listen, and to take action. Performative actions, rather than real change, will backfire. Talk about the things that matter to your customers from the point of view of the work you do for them.

Productivity & Mindset

Productivity begins with the physical health of your brain. Shift your perspective and focus on the things within your control to provide further productivity improvements. Create roles and expectations to better navigate working from home and with your life partner. Notice your energy and be open to new ways of solving the problems in your business. Take lessons from the work done to help those with ADHD. The focus is not the end result, but the steps you take to get there and how you take them including your mindset.

Technology

The pandemic and shift to work from home opened up new challenges in the world of cybersecurity. The best protection is a multilayered approach.

What is next?

The interviews continue and I invite you to join us at WhatBusinessesNeedToKnow.com to see the latest recommendations from experts across the globe. Connect with those experts and receive the support you need as you grow your business and navigate an ever-changing world. Subscribe to WhatBusinessesNeedToKnow.com/subscribe to receive these interviews delivered weekly to your inbox. If you have something you would like to share, submit an application at WhatBusinessesNeedToKnow.com/interview.

Acknowledgments

To Jennifer McGinley who saw this book well before I did and is the reason you are holding it in your hands.

To Robin Blackburn for the hours of time, energy, and thoughtfulness put into editing each interview so that they conveyed the message of the interviewee in a way that was easy to understand. Our timeline was short and yet you always were ahead of schedule. Thank you!

To Monica Molina for ensuring everyone always had the right information at the right time. You are the glue that holds Sappari Solutions, LLC together!

To Bob Graham for the inspiration for the interview series and for being my "first"! For being willing to test the waters, have conversations, and provide helpful feedback.

To the team at Write, Publish, Sell who put in the work that brought this book to fruition and connected with you, the reader.

To Joshua, Mira, and Evelyn, my children, for allowing the time I spent on evenings and weekends writing and editing when there were other things you would have preferred we do together.

For my husband, Jason, for his wonderfully critical eye that ensured that what was shared in this book was "right." I am thankful for his keen attention to detail and for his endurance in responding to my questions about covers, content, and more.

For my parents and sisters who have been supportive, excited, and encouraging of every project I have created.

For each and every person interviewed for being willing to share your expertise and experience to serve others.

About the Author

Nettie Owens is a certified, internationally recognized, and award-winning expert and speaker in the field of accountability and productivity. A graduate of Johns Hopkins University with a degree in Computer Science and a minor in Entrepreneurship and Management, Owens' methodologies are brain-based, researched, and backed by science. She received the designation of Certified Professional Organizer in Chronic Disorganization from the Institute for Challenging Disorganization.

Through training, speaking, coaching, blogging, and 86+ video interviews (at the time of this printing) on "What Businesses Need To Know Right Now," she brings over 17 years worth of experience to her clients, communities, and beyond. Owens has been featured on TLC, ABC, CNN, eHow FOX, YAHOO, World Economic Forum, and such publications as Authority Magazine, Parents, Entrepreneur, Tatler Hong Kong, and the Pittsburgh Gazette.

She works and writes from the hills north of Pittsburgh, Pennsylvania with her three children, husband, and their fur family. She balances her work with cooking, dancing, hiking, gardening, and travel when permitted.

Check out the interviews included in this book and connect with Nettie at www.whatbusinessesneedtoknow.com and www.nettieowens.com

Made in the USA
Middletown, DE
16 May 2021